THE MOTHER'S ALMANAC

CRISWELL FREEMAN

FAMILY
Christian Stores·

The quoted ideas expressed in this book (but not scripture verses) are not, in all cases, exact quotations, as some have been edited for clarity and brevity. In all cases, the author has attempted to maintain the speaker's original intent. In some cases, quoted material for this book was obtained from secondary sources, primarily print media. While every effort was made to ensure the accuracy of these sources, the accuracy cannot be guaranteed. For additions, deletions, corrections or clarifications in future editions of this text, please write FAMILY CHRISTIAN STORES.

Scripture quotations are taken from:

The Holy Bible, King James Version (KJV)

The Holy Bible, New International Version (NIV) Copyright © 1973, 1978, 1984, by International Bible Society. Used by permission of Zondervan Publishing House. All rights reserved.

The Holy Bible, New King James Version (NKJV) Copyright © 1982 by Thomas Nelson, Inc. Used by permission.

Holy Bible, New Living Translation, (NLT) copyright © 1996. Used by permission of Tyndale House Publishers, Inc., Wheaton, Illinois 60189. All rights reserved.

The Message (MSG)- This edition issued by contractual arrangement with NavPress, a division of The Navigators, U.S.A. Originally published by NavPress in English as THE MESSAGE: The Bible in Contemporary Language copyright 2002-2003 by Eugene Peterson. All rights reserved.

New Century Version®. (NCV) Copyright © 1987, 1988, 1991 by Word Publishing, a division of Thomas Nelson, Inc. All rights reserved. Used by permission.

The New American Standard Bible®, (NASB) Copyright © 1960, 1962, 1963, 1968, 1971, 1972, 1973, 1975, 1977, 1995 by The Lockman Foundation. Used by permission.

The Holman Christian Standard Bible™ (HCSB) Copyright © 1999, 2000, 2001 by Holman Bible Publishers. Used by permission.

Cover Design by Kim Russell / Wahoo Designs
Page Layout by Bart Dawson

ISBN 978-1-60587-008-3

THE MOTHER'S ALMANAC

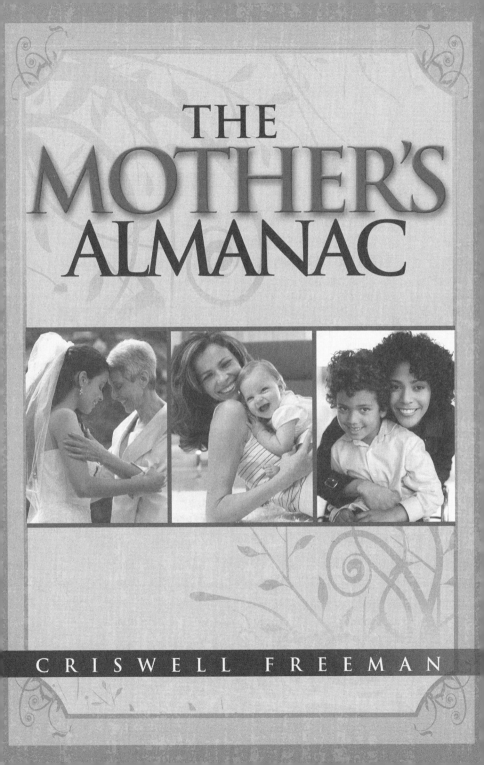

CRISWELL FREEMAN

TABLE OF CONTENTS

INTRODUCTION —7

1. THANKS, MOM —9

2. PEACE FOR THE JOURNEY —17

3. A JOYFUL SPIRIT —25

4. FAITH IN ACTION —33

5. THE POWER OF GOD'S WORD —39

6. OPTIMISM NOW —47

7. A MOTHER'S LOVE —55

8. LIVING ABOVE AND BEYOND REGRET —63

9. STRENGTH FOR THE JOURNEY —69

10. PRIORITIES FOR THE JOURNEY —77

11. HE RENEWS —83

12. SENSING GOD'S PRESENCE —89

13. FORGIVENESS NOW —95

14. TRUST HIM —101

15. THE POWER OF PATIENCE —109

16. CONTINUING TO GROW —117

17. THIS IS THE DAY —123

18. MAINTAINING PERSPECTIVE —129

19. ACCEPTING GOD'S ABUNDANCE —137

20. THANKSGIVING NOW —145

21. YOUR JOURNEY WITH GOD —153

22. HE WANTS YOU TO SERVE —159

23. GOD'S GIFT TO YOU: YOUR CHILDREN —165

24. DETOURS ON THE JOURNEY —173

25. THE RIGHT KIND OF EXAMPLE —181

26. THE POWER OF ENCOURAGEMENT —189

27. THE POWER OF ENTHUSIASM —197

28. YOUR SHEPHERD —203

29. BELIEVE IN YOURSELF! —211

30. ABOVE AND BEYOND WORRY —217

31. QUIET TIME WITH GOD —225

32. EMBRACED BY GOD —233

INTRODUCTION

Because you're reading this book, you probably answer to the name "Mom," "Mother," "Mommy," or some variation thereof—if so, congratulations. As a loving mother you have been blessed by your children and by your Creator.

In your hands you hold a handy almanac of great ideas for great moms like you. It contains essays, quotes, tips, Bible verses, and helpful hints that are intended to guide your path and lift your spirits.

Your life here on earth is an all-too-brief journey from the cradle to the grave. When you make that journey with God—and when you encourage your family members to do the same—you will avail yourself of the peace and abundance that God offers to those who invite Him into their hearts.

As a mother you are keenly aware of the priceless treasure that the Creator has entrusted to your care; that treasure, of course, is your family. And as a Christian, you're also aware of another incalculable treasure that is yours for the asking: the gift of eternal life that was purchased by God's only begotten Son on the cross at Calvary. This book serves as an inspirational reminder of these and other blessings that you, as a Christian mom, can savor for a lifetime and beyond.

Motherhood is both a priceless gift from God and an unrelenting responsibility. The ideas on these pages are intended to remind you that when it comes to the tough job of being a responsible mother, you and God, working together, are destined to do great things for your kids and for the world.

CHAPTER 1

THANKS, MOM

Her children rise up and call her blessed.

—

PROVERBS 31:28 NKJV

Dear Mom,

Thanks for the love, the care, the work, the discipline, the wisdom, the support, and the faith. Thanks for being a concerned parent and a worthy example. Thanks for giving life and for teaching it. Thanks for being patient with me, even when you were tired or frustrated—or both. Thanks for changing diapers and wiping away tears. And thanks for being a godly woman, one worthy of our admiration and our love.

You deserve a smile today, Mom, but you deserve so much more. You deserve our family's undying gratitude. And, you deserve God's love, His grace, and His peace. May you enjoy God's blessings always, and may you never, ever forget how much we love you.

Signed,

Your Family

MORE GREAT IDEAS ABOUT
OUR MOTHERS

A good woman is the best thing on earth. The church owes a debt to our faithful women which we can never estimate, to say nothing of the debt we owe in our homes to our godly wives and mothers.

VANCE HAVNER

Who can ever measure the benefit of a mother's inspiration?

CHARLES SWINDOLL

A person who has a praying mother has a most cherished possession.

BILLY GRAHAM

If you were blessed with a good mother, you will reap the benefits all of your days.

CHARLES SWINDOLL

A mother understands what her child doesn't say.

OLD SAYING

God wants to make something beautiful of our lives; our task—as God's children and as our children's parents—is to let Him.

JIM GALLERY

The mother is and must be, whether she knows it or not, the greatest, strongest, and most lasting teacher her children have.

HANNAH WHITALL SMITH

As a mother, my job is to take care of the possible and trust God with the impossible.

RUTH BELL GRAHAM

Being a full-time mom is the hardest job I've ever had, but it is also the best job I've ever had. The pay is lousy, but the rewards are eternal.

LISA WHELCHEL

A mother's arms are made of tenderness.

VICTOR HUGO

MORE WISDOM FROM GOD'S WORD

Don't withhold correction from a youth . . . .

PROVERBS 23:13 HCSB

Honor your father and your mother so that you may have a long life in the land that the Lord your God is giving you.

EXODUS 20:12 HCSB

Listen, my son, to your father's instruction, and don't reject your mother's teaching.

PROVERBS 1:8 HCSB

Let them first learn to show piety at home and to repay their parents; for this is good and acceptable before God.

1 TIMOTHY 5:4 NKJV

The LORD rewarded me according to my righteousness . . . .

PSALM 18:20 HCSB

A MOTHER IS

A mother is many things:

She is the giver of life and love,
    the maker of house and home.
She is chief cook and bottle washer,
    babysitter of last resort,
      provider,
        educator,
          doctor,
            disciplinarian,
              spiritual guide,
                counselor,
                  health inspector,
                    clothing consultant,
                      and taxi driver.

As she raises her children and cares for her family, a loving mother shapes eternity. Her legacy endures forever.

MORE GOOD IDEAS

A mother is the holiest thing alive.

SAMUEL TAYLOR COLERIDGE

What the mother sings to the cradle goes all the way down to the coffin.

HENRY WARD BEECHER

All that I am or hope to be I owe to my angel mother.

ABRAHAM LINCOLN

A TIMELY TIP

When you place your faith in God,
life becomes a grand adventure
energized by the power of God.

DEAR MOM,
On the Lines Below, Write Down Your Own Ideas About What It Means to Be a Mother

AND FINALLY . . .

DID YOU KNOW?

Anna Jarvis of Philadelphia began the campaign that brought about the official observance of Mother's Day in the United States. After her mother died, Anna wanted all mothers to be remembered. She asked that white carnations be the official mother's day symbol. And in 1914, President Woodrow Wilson signed the order that made Mother's Day a national holiday.

PEACE FOR THE JOURNEY

Peace I leave with you, My peace I give to you;
not as the world gives do I give to you.
Let not your heart be troubled, neither let it be afraid.

—

JOHN 14:27 NKJV

The beautiful words of John 14:27 give us hope: "Peace I leave with you, my peace I give to you . . . ." Jesus offers us peace, not as the world gives, but as He alone gives. We, as believers, can accept His peace or ignore it.

When we accept the peace of Jesus Christ into our hearts, our lives are transformed. And then, because we possess the gift of peace, we can share that gift with family members, friends, and fellow believers. If, on the other hand, we choose to ignore the gift of peace—for whatever reason—we cannot share it with others.

For busy mothers, a moment's peace can be a scarce commodity. But no matter how numerous the interruptions and demands of the day, God is ever-present, always ready and willing to offer comfort to those who seek "the peace that passes all understanding." How can we find the peace that we so desperately desire? By turning our days and our lives over to God. Elisabeth Elliot writes, "If my life is surrendered to God, all is well. Let me not grab it back, as though it were in peril in His hand but would be safer in mine!" May we, too, give our lives, our hopes, and our prayers to the Lord, and, by doing so, accept His will and His peace.

MORE GREAT IDEAS ABOUT PEACE

I believe that in every time and place it is within our power to acquiesce in the will of God—and what peace it brings to do so!

ELISABETH ELLIOT

To know God as He really is—in His essential nature and character—is to arrive at a citadel of peace that circumstances may storm, but can never capture.

CATHERINE MARSHALL

In the center of a hurricane there is absolute quiet and peace. There is no safer place than in the center of the will of God.

CORRIE TEN BOOM

When we do what is right, we have contentment, peace, and happiness.

BEVERLY LaHAYE

Peace does not mean to be in a place where there is no noise, trouble, or hard work. Peace means to be in the midst of all those things and still be calm in your heart.

CATHERINE MARSHALL

God is in control of history; it's His story. Doesn't that give you a great peace—especially when world events seem so tumultuous and insane?

KAY ARTHUR

The fruit of our placing all things in God's hands is the presence of His abiding peace in our hearts.

HANNAH WHITALL SMITH

We're prone to want God to change our circumstances, but He wants to change our character. We think that peace comes from the outside in, but it comes from the inside out.

WARREN WIERSBE

MORE WISDOM FROM GOD'S WORD

God has called us to peace.

1 CORINTHIANS 7:15 NKJV

Be of good comfort, be of one mind, live in peace; and the God of love and peace will be with you.

2 CORINTHIANS 13:11 NKJV

For He is our peace.

EPHESIANS 2:14 HCSB

The result of righteousness will be peace; the effect of righteousness will be quiet confidence forever.

ISAIAH 32:17 HCSB

Now the fruit of righteousness is sown in peace by those who make peace.

JAMES 3:18 NKJV

FINDING GENUINE CONTENTMENT

Everywhere we turn, or so it seems, the world promises us contentment and happiness. But the contentment that the world offers is fleeting and incomplete. Thankfully, the contentment that God offers is all encompassing and everlasting.

Happiness depends less upon our circumstances than upon our thoughts. When we turn our thoughts to God, to His gifts, and to His glorious creation, we experience the joy that God intends for His children. But, when we focus on the negative aspects of life—or when we disobey God's commandments—we cause ourselves needless suffering.

Do you sincerely want to be a contented Christian? Then set your mind and your heart upon God's love and His grace . . . and let Him take care of the rest.

MORE GOOD IDEAS

The key to contentment is to consider. Consider who you are and be satisfied with that. Consider what you have and be satisfied with that. Consider what God's doing and be satisfied with that.

LUCI SWINDOLL

When we are set free from the bondage of pleasing others, when we are free from currying others' favor and others' approval—then no one will be able to make us miserable or dissatisfied. And then, if we know we have pleased God, contentment will be our consolation.

KAY ARTHUR

Those who are God's without reserve are, in every sense, content.

HANNAH WHITALL SMITH

A TIMELY TIP

Contentment comes, not from your circumstances or your possessions, but from your attitude. And remember this: peace with God is the foundation of a contented life and a contented family.

DEAR MOM,
On the Lines Below, Write Down Your Own Ideas About God's Peace

AND FINALLY . . .

FAMILY LIFE IS THE FOUNDATION
OF HUMAN EXISTENCE,
AND MOTHER IS THE CORNERSTONE.

A JOYFUL SPIRIT

These things I have spoken to you, that My joy may remain in you, and that your joy may be full.

—

JOHN 15:11 NKJV

Are you a mom whose smile is evident for all to see? If so, congratulations: your joyful spirit serves as a powerful example to your family and friends. And because of your attitude, you may be assured that your children will indeed "rise up" and call you blessed (Proverbs 31:28).

Sometimes, amid the inevitable hustle and bustle of life here on earth, you may forfeit—albeit temporarily—the joy that God intends for you to experience and to share. But even on life's most difficult days, you may rest assured that God is in His heaven, and He still cares for you.

God's plan for you and your family includes heaping helpings of abundance and joy. Claim them. And remember that Christ offers you and your family priceless gifts: His abundance, His peace, and His joy. Accept those gifts and share them freely, just as Christ has freely shared Himself with you.

MORE GREAT IDEAS ABOUT
JOY

What is your focus today? Joy comes when it is Jesus first, others second . . . then you.

KAY ARTHUR

The Christian lifestyle is not one of legalistic do's and don'ts, but one that is positive, attractive, and joyful.

VONETTE BRIGHT

If you're a thinking Christian, you will be a joyful Christian.

MARIE T. FREEMAN

There may be no trumpet sound or loud applause when we make a right decision, just a calm sense of resolution and peace.

GLORIA GAITHER

Jesus did not promise to change the circumstances around us. He promised great peace and pure joy to those who would learn to believe that God actually controls all things.

CORRIE TEN BOOM

To a world that was spiritually dry and populated with parched lives scorched by sin, Jesus was the Living Water who would quench the thirsty soul, saving it from "bondage" and filling it with satisfaction and joy and purpose and meaning.

ANNE GRAHAM LOTZ

Joy is a by-product not of happy circumstances, education, or talent, but of a healthy relationship with God and a determination to love Him no matter what.

BARBARA JOHNSON

Unparalleled joy and victory come from allowing Christ to do "the hard thing" with us.

BETH MOORE

A life of intimacy with God is characterized by joy.

OSWALD CHAMBERS

Rejoice, the Lord is King; Your Lord and King adore! Rejoice, give thanks and sing and triumph evermore.

CHARLES WESLEY

MORE WISDOM FROM GOD'S WORD

Weeping may spend the night, but there is joy in the morning.

PSALM 30:5 HCSB

Rejoice in the Lord always. I will say it again: Rejoice!

PHILIPPIANS 4:4 HCSB

Make me to hear joy and gladness.

PSALM 51:8 KJV

Now I am coming to You, and I speak these things in the world so that they may have My joy completed in them.

JOHN 17:13 HCSB

A joyful heart makes a face cheerful.

PROVERBS 15:13 HCSB

HOW TO BE HAPPY

Happiness depends less upon our circumstances than upon our thoughts. When we turn our thoughts to God, to His gifts, and to His glorious creation, we experience the joy that God intends for His children. But, when we focus on the negative aspects of life, we inadvertently bring pain to our friends, to our families, and to ourselves.

Do you sincerely want to be a happy person? Then set your mind and your heart upon God's love and His grace. Seek a genuine, intimate, life-altering relationship with your Creator by studying His Word and trusting His promises. And while you're at it, count your blessings instead of your hardships. Then, after you've done these things, claim the joy, the peace, and the spiritual abundance that the Shepherd offers His sheep.

MORE GOOD IDEAS

If our hearts have been attuned to God through an abiding faith in Christ, the result will be joyous optimism and good cheer.

BILLY GRAHAM

I became aware of one very important concept I had missed before: my attitude—not my circumstances—was what was making me unhappy.

VONETTE BRIGHT

We will never be happy until we make God the source of our fulfillment and the answer to our longings.

STORMIE OMARTIAN

A TIMELY TIP

Joy is contagious. Remember that a joyful family starts with joyful parents.

DEAR MOM,
On the Lines Below, Write Down Your Own Ideas About Joy

AND FINALLY . . .

SMILE—IT INCREASES YOUR FACE VALUE.

CHAPTER 4

FAITH IN ACTION

For whatever is born of God overcomes the world.
And this is the victory that has overcome the world—our faith.

—

1 JOHN 5:4 NKJV

Are you a mother whose faith is evident for all to see? Do you trust God's promises without reservation, or do you question His promises without hesitation?

Every life—including yours—is a series of successes and failures, celebrations and disappointments, joys and sorrows. Every step of the way, through every triumph and tragedy, God will stand by your side and strengthen you . . . if you have faith in Him.

Jesus taught His disciples that if they had faith, they could move mountains. You can, too, and so can your family. But you must have faith. So today and every day, trust your Heavenly Father, praise the sacrifice of His Son . . . and then let the mountain-moving begin.

MORE GREAT IDEAS ABOUT
FAITH

Faith is seeing light with the eyes of your heart, when the eyes of your body see only darkness.

BARBARA JOHNSON

Grace calls you to get up, throw off your blanket of helplessness, and to move on through life in faith.

KAY ARTHUR

Just as our faith strengthens our prayer life, so do our prayers deepen our faith. Let us pray often, starting today, for a deeper, more powerful faith.

SHIRLEY DOBSON

Faith does not concern itself with the entire journey. One step is enough.

MRS. CHARLES E. COWMAN

Faith is nothing more or less than actively trusting God.

CATHERINE MARSHALL

When you and I place our faith in Jesus Christ and invite Him to come live within us, the Holy Spirit comes upon us, and the power of God overshadows us, and the life of Jesus is born within us.

ANNE GRAHAM LOTZ

There are a lot of things in life that are difficult to understand. Faith allows the soul to go beyond what the eyes can see.

JOHN MAXWELL

Nothing is more disastrous than to study faith, analyze faith, make noble resolves of faith, but never actually to make the leap of faith.

VANCE HAVNER

If God chooses to remain silent, faith is content.

RUTH BELL GRAHAM

MORE WISDOM FROM GOD'S WORD

Now faith is the reality of what is hoped for, the proof of what is not seen.

HEBREWS 11:1 HCSB

Now without faith it is impossible to please God, for the one who draws near to Him must believe that He exists and rewards those who seek Him.

HEBREWS 11:6 HCSB

For we walk by faith, not by sight.

2 CORINTHIANS 5:7 HCSB

If you do not stand firm in your faith, then you will not stand at all.

ISAIAH 7:9 HCSB

Indeed, God is my salvation. I will trust [Him] and not be afraid. Because Yah, the LORD, is my strength and my song, He has become my salvation.

ISAIAH 12:2 HCSB

MORE GOOD IDEAS

Worry and anxiety are sand in the machinery of life; faith is the oil.

E. STANLEY JONES

Our only means of living in Him is by faith, so trusting Him to see us through any and all trials and testings delights our Lord!

BILL BRIGHT

Sometimes the very essence of faith is trusting God in the midst of things He knows good and well we cannot comprehend.

BETH MOORE

A TIMELY TIP

Faith in God is contagious, and when it comes to your family's spiritual journey, no one's faith is more contagious than yours! Act, pray, praise, and trust God with the certain knowledge that every member of your family is watching . . . carefully!

DEAR MOM,
On the Lines Below, Write Down Your Own Ideas About
The Power of Faith

CHAPTER 5

THE POWER OF GOD'S WORD

Heaven and earth will pass away,
but My words will never pass away.

—

MATTHEW 24:35 HCSB

God's Word is unlike any other book. The Bible is a roadmap for life here on earth and for life eternal. As Christians, we are called upon to study God's Holy Word, to trust His Word, to follow its commandments, and to share its Good News with the world.

The words of Matthew 4:4 remind us that, "Man shall not live by bread alone but by every word that proceedeth out of the mouth of God" (KJV). As believers, we must study the Bible and meditate upon its meaning for our lives. Otherwise, we deprive ourselves of a priceless gift from our Creator.

Warren Wiersbe observed, "When the child of God looks into the Word of God, he sees the Son of God. And, he is transformed by the Spirit of God to share in the glory of God." God's Holy Word is, indeed, a transforming, life-changing, one-of-a-kind treasure. And, a passing acquaintance with the Good Book is insufficient for Christians who seek to obey God's Word and to understand His will. After all, man—and mom—do not live by bread alone . . .

MORE GREAT IDEAS ABOUT GOD'S WORD

I need the spiritual revival that comes from spending quiet time alone with Jesus in prayer and in thoughtful meditation on His Word.

ANNE GRAHAM LOTZ

The Bible became a living book and a guide for my life.

VONETTE BRIGHT

Words fail to express my love for this holy Book, my gratitude for its author, for His love and goodness. How shall I thank him for it?

LOTTIE MOON

If we are not continually fed with God's Word, we will starve spiritually.

STORMIE OMARTIAN

Weave the unveiling fabric of God's Word through your heart and mind. It will hold strong, even if the rest of life unravels.

GIGI GRAHAM TCHIVIDJIAN

God can see clearly no matter how dark or foggy the night is. Trust His Word to guide you safely home.

LISA WHELCHEL

God's Word is a light not only to our path but also to our thinking. Place it in your heart today, and you will never walk in darkness.

JONI EARECKSON TADA

Walking in faith brings you to the Word of God. There you will be healed, cleansed, fed, nurtured, equipped, and matured.

KAY ARTHUR

God has given us all sorts of counsel and direction in his written Word; thank God, we have it written down in black and white.

JOHN ELDREDGE

MORE WISDOM FROM GOD'S WORD

But the word of the Lord endures forever. And this is the word that was preached as the gospel to you.

1 PETER 1:25 HCSB

All Scripture is inspired by God and is profitable for teaching, for rebuking, for correcting, for training in righteousness, so that the man of God may be complete, equipped for every good work.

2 TIMOTHY 3:16-17 HCSB

For the word of God is living and effective and sharper than any two-edged sword, penetrating as far as to divide soul, spirit, joints, and marrow; it is a judge of the ideas and thoughts of the heart.

HEBREWS 4:12 HCSB

The one who is from God listens to God's words. This is why you don't listen, because you are not from God.

JOHN 8:47 HCSB

Every word of God is pure; He is a shield to those who put their trust in Him.

PROVERBS 30:5 NKJV

MAKE TIME FOR GOD

If you ever find that you're simply "too busy" for a daily chat with your Father in heaven, it's time to take a long, hard look at your priorities and your values. Each day has 1,440 minutes—do you value your relationship with God enough to spend a few of those minutes with Him? He deserves that much of your time and more—is He receiving it from you? Hopefully so.

As you consider your plans for the day ahead, here's a tip: organize your life around this simple principle: "God first." When you place your Creator where He belongs—at the very center of your day and your life—the rest of your priorities will fall into place.

MORE GOOD IDEAS

God is a place of safety you can run to, but it helps if you are running to Him on a daily basis so that you are in familiar territory.

STORMIE OMARTIAN

God calls us to seek him daily in order to serve him daily.

SHEILA CRAGG

A quiet morning with a loving God puts the events of the upcoming day into proper perspective.

JANETTE OKE

A TIMELY TIP

Charles Swindoll writes, "There are four words I wish we would never forget, and they are, 'God keeps his word.'" And remember: When it comes to studying God's Word, school is always in session.

DEAR MOM,
On the Lines Below, Write Down Your Own Ideas About The Importance of Studying God's Word

AND FINALLY . . .

IF YOUR BIBLE IS FALLING APART,
CHANCES ARE YOUR LIFE IS
STAYING TOGETHER.

CHAPTER 6

OPTIMISM NOW

*Finally brothers, whatever is true, whatever is honorable,
whatever is just, whatever is pure, whatever is lovely,
whatever is commendable—if there is any moral excellence
and if there is any praise—dwell on these things.*

—

PHILIPPIANS 4:8 HCSB

Because you are a conscientious mom living in a difficult world, you may find yourself pulled down by the inevitable demands and worries of everyday life in the 21st century. Ours is a world brimming with temptations, distractions, and dangers. Sometimes, we can't help ourselves: we worry for our families, and we worry for ourselves.

If you become discouraged, exhausted, or both, then it's time to take your concerns to God. Whether you find yourself at the pinnacle of the mountain or the darkest depths of the valley, God is there. Open your heart to Him and He will lift your spirits and renew your strength.

Today, as a gift to your family and yourself, why not claim the joy that is rightfully yours in Christ? Why not take time to celebrate God's glorious creation? Why not trust your hopes instead of your fears? When you do, you will think optimistically about yourself and your world . . . and you can then share your optimism with others. They'll be better for it, and so will you. But not necessarily in that order.

MORE GREAT IDEAS ABOUT OPTIMISM

Gratitude unlocks the fullness of life. It turns what we have into enough, and more. It turns denial into acceptance, chaos to order, confusion to clarity. It can turn a meal into a feast, a house into a home, a stranger into a friend. Gratitude makes sense of our past, brings peace for today, and creates a vision for tomorrow.

MELODY BEATTIE

If you can't tell whether your glass is half-empty or half-full, you don't need another glass; what you need is better eyesight . . . and a more thankful heart.

MARIE T. FREEMAN

Make the least of all that goes and the most of all that comes. Don't regret what is past. Cherish what you have. Look forward to all that is to come. And most important of all, rely moment by moment on Jesus Christ.

GIGI GRAHAM TCHIVIDJIAN

When you affirm big, believe big, and pray big, big things happen.

NORMAN VINCENT PEALE

The Christian lifestyle is not one of legalistic do's and don'ts, but one that is positive, attractive, and joyful.

VONETTE BRIGHT

Developing a positive attitude means working continually to find what is uplifting and encouraging.

BARBARA JOHNSON

We may run, walk, stumble, drive, or fly, but let us never lose sight of the reason for the journey, or miss a chance to see a rainbow on the way.

GLORIA GAITHER

Feelings of confidence depend upon the type of thoughts you habitually occupy. Think defeat, and you are bound to be defeated.

NORMAN VINCENT PEALE

MORE WISDOM FROM GOD'S WORD

Make me hear joy and gladness.

PSALM 51:8 NKJV

My cup runs over. Surely goodness and mercy shall follow me all the days of my life; and I will dwell in the house of the Lord Forever.

PSALM 23:5-6 NKJV

But if we hope for what we do not see, we eagerly wait for it with patience.

ROMANS 8:25 HCSB

For God has not given us a spirit of fearfulness, but one of power, love, and sound judgment.

2 TIMOTHY 1:7 HCSB

Be strong and courageous, all you who put your hope in the LORD.

PSALM 31:24 HCSB

DEFEATING PESSIMISM

Pessimism is intellectual poison. And negativity has the power to harm your heart if you let it. So if you've allowed negative thoughts to creep into your mind and heart, here's your assignment: Start spending more time thinking about your blessings and less time fretting about your hardships.

This day, like every other, is a gift from God, filled to the brim with possibilities. But persistent pessimistic thoughts can rob you of the energy you need to accomplish the most important tasks on your to-do list. So today, be careful to direct your thoughts toward things positive. And while you're at it, take time to thank the Giver of all things good for gifts that are, in truth, far too numerous to count.

Don't miss the beautiful colors
of the rainbow
while you're looking for the
pot of gold at the end of it!

—

BARBARA JOHNSON

MORE GOOD IDEAS

To lose heart is to lose everything.

JOHN ELDREDGE

We never get anywhere—nor do our conditions and circumstances change—when we look at the dark side of life.

MRS. CHARLES E. COWMAN

A pessimist is someone who believes that when her cup runneth over she'll need a mop.

BARBARA JOHNSON

A TIMELY TIP

If your thoughts tend toward the negative end of the spectrum, redirect them. How? You can start by counting your blessings and by thanking your Father in heaven. And while you're at it, train yourself to begin thinking thoughts that are more rational, more accepting, and more upbeat (Philippians 4:8) . . . for your children's sake.

DEAR MOM,
On the Lines Below, Write Down Your Own Ideas About The Power of Optimism

AND FINALLY . . .

A MOTHER'S LOVE
SEES NO IMPOSSIBILITIES.

CHAPTER 7

A MOTHER'S LOVE

Now these three remain: faith, hope, and love.
But the greatest of these is love.

—

1 CORINTHIANS 13:13 HCSB

Few things in life are as precious or as enduring as a mother's love. Our mothers give us life, and they care for us. They nurture us when we are sick and encourage us when we're brokenhearted. Indeed, a mother's love is both powerful and priceless.

The words of 1st Corinthians 13 remind us that faith is important; so, too, is hope. But love is more important still. Christ showed His love for us on the cross, and, as Christians, we are called upon to return Christ's love by sharing it. Sometimes love is easy (puppies and sleeping children come to mind), and sometimes love is hard (fallible human beings come to mind). But God's Word is clear: We are to love our families and our neighbors without reservation or condition.

As a caring mother, you are not only shaping the lives of your loved ones; you are also, in a very real sense, reshaping eternity. It's a big job, a job so big, in fact, that God saw fit to entrust it to some of the most important people in His kingdom: loving moms like you.

MORE GREAT IDEAS ABOUT
LOVE

The mother is and must be, whether she knows it or not, the greatest, strongest, and most lasting teacher her children have.

HANNAH WHITALL SMITH

There is no more influential or powerful role on earth than a mother's.

CHARLES SWINDOLL

As a mother, my job is to take care of the possible and trust God with the impossible.

RUTH BELL GRAHAM

Love always means sacrifice.

ELISABETH ELLIOT

Prayer is the ultimate love language. It communicates in ways we can't.

STORMIE OMARTIAN

Love is something like the clouds that were in the sky before the sun came out. You cannot touch the clouds, you know; but you feel the rain and know how glad the flowers and the thirsty earth are to have it after a hot day. You cannot touch love either; but you feel the sweetness that it pours into everything.

ANNIE SULLIVAN

Agape is a kind of love God demonstrates to one person through another.

BETH MOORE

Forgiveness is the precondition of love.

CATHERINE MARSHALL

Maternal love: a miraculous substance which God multiplies as he divides it.

VICTOR HUGO

Mother's love grows by giving.

CHARLES LAMB

MORE WISDOM FROM GOD'S WORD

I pray that you, being rooted and firmly established in love, may be able to comprehend with all the saints what is the breadth and width, height and depth, and to know the Messiah's love that surpasses knowledge, so you may be filled with all the fullness of God.

EPHESIANS 3:17-19 HCSB

If I speak the languages of men and of angels, but do not have love, I am a sounding gong or a clanging cymbal.

1 CORINTHIANS 13:1 HCSB

Dear friends, if God loved us in this way, we also must love one another.

1 JOHN 4:11 HCSB

We love because He first loved us.

1 JOHN 4:19 HCSB

Above all, keep your love for one another at full strength, since love covers a multitude of sins.

1 PETER 4:8 HCSB

ON LOVING AND LISTENING

For many parents, the temptation to lecture their children is almost irresistible. But oftentimes, it's more helpful to listen than to lecture.

God's Word instructs us to be quick to listen and slow to speak. And when it comes to the important job of raising the next generation and strengthening our families, we're wise to listen carefully (first) and then offer helpful words (next).

Perhaps God gave us two ears and one mouth for a reason: so that we might listen twice as much as we speak. After all, listening quietly to our kids can be a wonderful form of encouragement. Besides, after we've listened carefully to our youngsters, we're more likely to respond wisely, not impulsively.

So remember that, as a parent, you have the power to guide your child with your words and your ears. And remember that the words you don't speak can be just as helpful as the ones you do speak. So talk—and listen—accordingly.

MORE GOOD IDEAS

Listening is loving.

ZIG ZIGLAR

The failure to listen might be the biggest hindrance of all to family communications.

ED YOUNG

The cliché is true: People don't care what we know until they know we care.

RICK WARREN

A TIMELY TIP

Children form their ideas about God's love by experiencing their parents' love. Live—and love—accordingly.

DEAR MOM,
On the Lines Below, Write Down Your Own Ideas About
Love

AND FINALLY . . .

DID YOU KNOW?

In the United States, the likelihood of a mother delivering twins in 2005 was about 1 in 32. Her chances of delivering triplets was approximately 1 in 618.

CHAPTER 8

LIVING ABOVE AND BEYOND REGRET

*One thing I do, forgetting those things which are behind
and reaching forward to those things which are ahead,
I press toward the goal for the prize of the upward call
of God in Christ Jesus.*

—

PHILIPPIANS 3:13-14 NKJV

Bitterness can destroy you if you let it . . . so don't let it! If you are caught up in intense feelings of anger or regret, you know all too well the destructive power of these emotions. How can you rid yourself of these feelings? First, you must prayerfully ask God to free you from these feelings. Then, you must learn to catch yourself whenever thoughts of bitterness begin to attack you. Your challenge is this: You must learn to resist negative thoughts before they hijack your emotions.

Barbara Johnson has this sound advice: "It is better to forgive and forget than to resent and remember." And she's right—it's better to forget than regret.

MORE GREAT IDEAS ABOUT
REGRET

Get rid of the poison of built-up anger and the acid of long-term resentment.

CHARLES SWINDOLL

Our yesterdays present irreparable things to us; it is true that we have lost opportunities which will never return, but God can transform this destructive anxiety into a constructive thoughtfulness for the future. Let the past sleep, but let it sleep on the bosom of Christ. Leave the Irreparable Past in His hands, and step out into the Irresistible Future with Him.

OSWALD CHAMBERS

In the Christian story God descends to reascend. He comes down; . . . down to the very roots and sea-bed of the Nature he has created. But He goes down to come up again and bring the whole ruined world with Him.

C. S. LEWIS

He is ever faithful and gives us the song in the night to soothe our spirits and fresh joy each morning to lift our souls. What a marvelous Lord!

BILL BRIGHT

The enemy of our souls loves to taunt us with past failures, wrongs, disappointments, disasters, and calamities. And if we let him continue doing this, our life becomes a long and dark tunnel, with very little light at the end.

CHARLES SWINDOLL

Sold for thirty pieces of silver, he redeemed the world.

R. G. LEE

For God is not merely mending, not simply restoring a status quo. Redeemed humanity is to be something more glorious than unfallen humanity.

C. S. LEWIS

There is no road back to yesterday.

OSWALD CHAMBERS

Discontent dries up the soul.

ELISABETH ELLIOT

No matter what, don't ever let yesterday use up too much of today.

BARBARA JOHNSON

MORE WISDOM FROM GOD'S WORD

Do not remember the past events, pay no attention to things of old. Look, I am about to do something new; even now it is coming. Do you not see it? Indeed, I will make a way in the wilderness, rivers in the desert.

ISAIAH 43:18-19 HCSB

Should we accept only good from God and not adversity?

JOB 2:10 HCSB

Consider it a great joy, my brothers, whenever you experience various trials, knowing that the testing of your faith produces endurance. But endurance must do its complete work, so that you may be mature and complete, lacking nothing.

JAMES 1:2-4 HCSB

And don't be wishing you were someplace else or with someone else. Where you are right now is God's place for you. Live and obey and love and believe right there.

1 CORINTHIANS 7:17 MSG

MORE GOOD IDEAS

Reflect upon your present blessings, of which every man has many—not on your past misfortunes, of which all men have some.

CHARLES DICKENS

Regret is an appalling waste of energy; you can't build on it; it is good only for wallowing.

KATHERINE MANSFIELD

To be happy, drop the words "if only," and substitute instead the words "next time."

SMILEY BLANTON

A TIMELY TIP

Avoid self-pity and renounce regret. Feeling sorry for yourself is a waste of precious time and energy; regretting the mistakes of yesterday won't help you build a better tomorrow.

DEAR MOM,
On the Lines Below, Write Down Your Own Ideas About Making Peace with the Past

CHAPTER 9

STRENGTH FOR THE JOURNEY

*And He said to me, "My grace is sufficient for you,
for My strength is made perfect in weakness."*

—

2 CORINTHIANS 12:9 NKJV

If you're a mother with too many demands and too few hours in which to meet them, you are not alone. Motherhood is perhaps the world's most demanding profession. But don't fret: even when it seems that your responsibilities are simply too great to bear, you and God, working together, can handle them. So focus not upon the difficulties of your circumstances, but instead upon God and upon His love for you. Then, ask Him for the strength that you need to fulfill your daily duties.

When you turn your thoughts and prayers to your Heavenly Father, He will give you the energy and the perspective to complete the most important items on your to-do list. And then, once you've done your best, leave the rest up to God. He can handle it . . . and will.

MORE GREAT IDEAS ABOUT STRENGTH

When the dream of our heart is one that God has planted there, a strange happiness flows into us. At that moment, all of the spiritual resources of the universe are released to help us. Our praying is then at one with the will of God and becomes a channel for the Creator's purposes for us and our world.

CATHERINE MARSHALL

God does not dispense strength and encouragement like a druggist fills your prescription. The Lord doesn't promise to give us something to take so we can handle our weary moments. He promises us Himself. That is all. And that is enough.

CHARLES SWINDOLL

Worry does not empty tomorrow of its sorrow; it empties today of its strength.

CORRIE TEN BOOM

The power of God through His Spirit will work within us to the degree that we permit it.

MRS. CHARLES E. COWMAN

One reason so much American Christianity is a mile wide and an inch deep is that Christians are simply tired. Sometimes you need to kick back and rest for Jesus' sake.

DENNIS SWANBERG

Sometimes I think spiritual and physical strength is like manna: you get just what you need for the day, no more.

SUZANNE DALE EZELL

When you and I are related to Jesus Christ, our strength and wisdom and peace and joy and love and hope may run out, but His life rushes in to keep us filled to the brim. We are showered with blessings, not because of anything we have or have not done, but simply because of Him.

ANNE GRAHAM LOTZ

We are never stronger than the moment we admit we are weak.

BETH MOORE

Hope can give us life. It can provide energy that would otherwise do us in completely if we tried to operate in our own strength.

BARBARA JOHNSON

MORE WISDOM FROM GOD'S WORD

You, therefore, my child, be strong in the grace that is in Christ Jesus.

2 TIMOTHY 2:1 HCSB

The Lord is my strength and my song; He has become my salvation.

EXODUS 15:2 HCSB

He gives strength to the weary and strengthens the powerless.

ISAIAH 40:29 HCSB

But those who wait on the Lord Shall renew their strength; They shall mount up with wings like eagles, They shall run and not be weary, They shall walk and not faint.

ISAIAH 40:31 NKJV

Finally, be strengthened by the Lord and by His vast strength.

EPHESIANS 6:10 HCSB

INFINITE POSSIBILITIES

Ours is a God of infinite possibilities. But sometimes, because of limited faith and limited understanding, we wrongly assume that God cannot or will not intervene in the affairs of mankind. Such assumptions are simply wrong.

Are you afraid to ask God to do big things in your life? Is your faith threadbare and worn? If so, it's time to abandon your doubts and reclaim your faith in God's promises.

God's Word makes it clear: absolutely nothing is impossible for the Lord. And since the Bible means what it says, you can be comforted in the knowledge that the Creator of the universe can do miraculous things in your own life and in the lives of your loved ones. Your challenge, Mom, is to take God at His word and to expect the miraculous. When you do your part, He will most assuredly do His.

MORE GOOD IDEAS

If we take God's program, we can have God's power—not otherwise.

E. STANLEY JONES

No giant will ever be a match for a big God with a little rock.

BETH MOORE

He has transforming power. He can change the quality of our lives.

CHARLES SWINDOLL

A TIMELY TIP

Feeling exhausted? Try this: Start getting more sleep each night; begin a program of regular, sensible exercise; avoid harmful food and drink; and turn your problems over to God . . . and the greatest of these is "turn your problems over to God."

DEAR MOM,
On the Lines Below, Write Down Your Own Ideas About Finding Strength

And Finally . . .

Life is fragile—handle with prayer.

CHAPTER 10

PRIORITIES FOR THE JOURNEY

He said to them all, "If anyone desires to come after Me,
let him deny himself, and take up his cross daily,
and follow Me. For whoever desires to save his life will lose it,
but whoever loses his life for My sake will save it."

—

LUKE 9:23-24 NKJV

First things first. These words are easy to speak but hard to put into practice, especially for busy mothers. Why? Because so many people are tugging on mom's apron strings (either literally or figuratively).

If you're having trouble prioritizing your day, perhaps you've been trying to organize your life according to your own plans, not God's. A better strategy, of course, is to take your daily obligations and place them in the hands of the One who created you. To do so, you must prioritize your day according to God's commandments, and you must seek His will and His wisdom in all matters. Then, you can face the day with the assurance that the same God who created our universe out of nothingness will help you place first things first in your own life.

Do you feel overwhelmed or confused? Turn the concerns

of this day over to a higher Source. Then, listen for His answer . . . and trust the answer He gives.

MORE GREAT IDEAS ABOUT PRIORITIES

It's sobering to contemplate how much time, effort, sacrifice, compromise, and attention we give to acquiring and increasing our supply of something that is totally insignificant in eternity.

ANNE GRAHAM LOTZ

Great relief and satisfaction can come from seeking God's priorities for us in each season, discerning what is "best" in the midst of many noble opportunities, and pouring our most excellent energies into those things.

BETH MOORE

Our leisure, even our play, is a matter of serious concern. There is no neutral ground in the universe: every square inch, every split second, is claimed by God and counterclaimed by Satan.

C. S. LEWIS

Sin is largely a matter of mistaken priorities. Any sin in us that is cherished, hidden, and not confessed will cut the nerve center of our faith.

CATHERINE MARSHALL

Have you prayed about your resources lately? Find out how God wants you to use your time and your money. No matter what it costs, forsake all that is not of God.

KAY ARTHUR

There were endless demands on Jesus' time. Still he was able to make that amazing claim of "completing the work you gave me to do." (John 17:4 NIV)

ELISABETH ELLIOT

We set our eyes on the finish line, forgetting the past, and straining toward the mark of spiritual maturity and fruitfulness.

VONETTE BRIGHT

The manifold rewards of a serious, consistent prayer life demonstrate clearly that time with our Lord should be our first priority.

SHIRLEY DOBSON

MORE WISDOM FROM GOD'S WORD

And I pray this: that your love will keep on growing in knowledge and every kind of discernment, so that you can determine what really matters and can be pure and blameless in the day of Christ.

PHILIPPIANS 1:9 HCSB

He said to them all, "If anyone desires to come after Me, let him deny himself, and take up his cross daily, and follow Me. For whoever desires to save his life will lose it, but whoever loses his life for My sake will save it."

LUKE 9:23-24 NKJV

Now it happened as they went that He entered a certain village; and a certain woman named Martha welcomed Him into her house. And she had a sister called Mary, who also sat at Jesus' feet and heard His word. But Martha was distracted with much serving, and she approached Him and said, "Lord, do You not care that my sister has left me to serve alone? Therefore tell her to help me." And Jesus answered and said to her, "Martha, Martha, you are worried and troubled about many things. But one thing is needed, and Mary has chosen that good part, which will not be taken away from her."

LUKE 10:38-42 NKJV

MORE GOOD IDEAS

You can't get second things by putting them first; you can get second things only by putting first things first.

C. S. LEWIS

Setting goals is one way you can be sure that you will focus your efforts on the main things so that trivial matters will not become your focus.

CHARLES STANLEY

How important it is for us—young and old—to live as if Jesus would return any day—to set our goals, make our choices, raise our children, and conduct business with the perspective of the imminent return of our Lord.

GLORIA GAITHER

A TIMELY TIP

Unless you put first things first, you're bound to finish last. And don't forget that putting first things first means God first and family next.

DEAR MOM,
On the Lines Below, Write Down Your Own Ideas About Establishing the Right Priorities

CHAPTER 11

HE RENEWS

I will give you a new heart and put a new spirit within you.

—

EZEKIEL 36:26 HCSB

God intends that His children lead joyous lives filled with abundance and peace. But sometimes, as all mothers can attest, abundance and peace seem very far away. It is then that we must turn to God for renewal, and when we do, He will restore us.

Have you "tapped in" to the power of God, or are you muddling along under your own power? If you are weary, worried, fretful, or fearful, then it is time to turn to a strength much greater than your own.

The Bible tells us that we can do all things through the power of our risen Savior, Jesus Christ. Our challenge, then, is clear: we must place Christ where He belongs: at the very center of our lives.

Are you tired or troubled? Turn your heart toward God in prayer. Are you weak or worried? Make the time to delve deeply into God's Holy Word. When you do, you'll discover that the Creator of the universe stands ready and able to create a new sense of wonderment and joy in you.

MORE GREAT IDEAS ABOUT RENEWAL

He is the God of wholeness and restoration.

STORMIE OMARTIAN

Repentance removes old sins and wrong attitudes, and it opens the way for the Holy Spirit to restore our spiritual health.

SHIRLEY DOBSON

God specializes in things fresh and firsthand. His plans for you this year may outshine those of the past. He's prepared to fill your days with reasons to give Him praise.

JONI EARECKSON TADA

Whoever you are, whatever your condition or circumstance, whatever your past or problem, Jesus can restore you to wholeness.

ANNE GRAHAM LOTZ

Troubles we bear trustfully can bring us a fresh vision of God and a new outlook on life, an outlook of peace and hope.

BILLY GRAHAM

How motivating it has been for me to view my early morning devotions as time of retreat alone with Jesus, Who desires that I "come with Him by myself to a quiet place" in order to pray, read His Word, listen for His voice, and be renewed in my spirit.

ANNE GRAHAM LOTZ

When we invite Jesus into our lives, we experience life in the fullest, most vital sense.

CATHERINE MARSHALL

Jesus is calling the weary to rest, / Calling today, calling today, / Bring Him your burden and you shall be blest; / He will not turn you away.

FANNY CROSBY

For centuries now, Christians have poured out their hearts to the Lord and found treasured moments of refuge.

BILL HYBELS

Walking with God leads to receiving his intimate counsel, and counseling leads to deep restoration.

JOHN ELDREDGE

MORE WISDOM FROM GOD'S WORD

But may the God of all grace, who called us to His eternal glory by Christ Jesus, after you have suffered a while, perfect, establish, strengthen, and settle you.

1 PETER 5:10 NKJV

Finally, brothers, rejoice. Be restored, be encouraged, be of the same mind, be at peace, and the God of love and peace will be with you.

2 CORINTHIANS 13:11 HCSB

But those who wait on the Lord shall renew their strength; they shall mount up with wings like eagles, they shall run and not be weary, they shall walk and not faint.

ISAIAH 40:31 NKJV

Therefore if anyone is in Christ, he is a new creature; the old things passed away; behold, new things have come.

2 CORINTHIANS 5:17 HCSB

Do not remember the former things, nor consider the things of old. Behold, I will do a new thing.

ISAIAH 43:18-19 NKJV

MORE GOOD IDEAS

If you've found yourself breathlessly chasing the guy in front of you, break free. Spend some time with your family. Take a walk with someone you love. Hold a three-year-old on your lap and tell him or her a story. Life is simply too short to be spent plodding around in endless circles.

JAMES DOBSON

Let's face it. None of us can do a thousand things to the glory of God. And, in our own vain attempt to do so, we stand the risk of forfeiting a precious thing.

BETH MOORE

The same voice that brought Lazarus out of the tomb raised us to newness of life.

C. H. SPURGEON

A TIMELY TIP

Do you need time for yourself? Take it. Ruth Bell Graham observed, "It is important that we take time out for ourselves—for relaxation, for refreshment." Enough said.

DEAR MOM,
On the Lines Below, Write Down Your Own Ideas About
The Need to Recharge Our Batteries

CHAPTER 12

SENSING GOD'S PRESENCE

Draw near to God, and He will draw near to you.

—

JAMES 4:8 HCSB

I f you are a busy mother with more obligations than you have time to count, you know all too well that the demands of everyday life can, on occasion, seem overwhelming. Thankfully, even on the days when you feel overburdened, overworked, overstressed, and under-appreciated, God is trying to get His message through . . . your job is to listen.

Are you tired, discouraged, or fearful? Be comforted because God is with you. Are you confused? Listen to the quiet voice of your Heavenly Father. Are you bitter? Talk with God and seek His guidance. In whatever condition you find yourself—whether you are happy or sad, victorious or vanquished, troubled or triumphant—carve out moments of silent solitude to celebrate God's gifts and to experience His presence.

The familiar words of Psalm 46:10 remind us to be still before the Creator. When we do, we encounter the awesome presence of our loving Heavenly Father, and we are comforted in the knowledge that God is not just near. He is here.

MORE GREAT IDEAS ABOUT GOD'S PRESENCE

Our souls were made to live in an upper atmosphere, and we stifle and choke if we live on any lower level. Our eyes were made to look off from these heavenly heights, and our vision is distorted by any lower gazing.

HANNAH WHITALL SMITH

Through the death and broken body of Jesus Christ on the Cross, you and I have been given access to the presence of God when we approach Him by faith in prayer.

ANNE GRAHAM LOTZ

If you want to hear God's voice clearly and you are uncertain, then remain in His presence until He changes that uncertainty. Often, much can happen during this waiting for the Lord. Sometimes, He changes pride into humility, doubt into faith and peace.

CORRIE TEN BOOM

Give yourself a gift today: be present with yourself. God is. Enjoy your own personality. God does.

BARBARA JOHNSON

It is God to whom and with whom we travel, and while He is the End of our journey, He is also at every stopping place.

ELISABETH ELLIOT

If your heart has grown cold, it is because you have moved away from the fire of His presence.

BETH MOORE

God wants to be in our leisure time as much as He is in our churches and in our work.

BETH MOORE

Oh! what a Savior, gracious to all, / Oh! how His blessings round us fall, / Gently to comfort, kindly to cheer, / Sleeping or waking, God is near.

FANNY CROSBY

The world, space, and all visible components reverberate with God's Presence and demonstrate His Mighty Power.

FRANKLIN GRAHAM

MORE WISDOM FROM GOD'S WORD

You will seek Me and find Me when you search for Me with all your heart.

JEREMIAH 29:13 HCSB

The Lord is near all who call out to Him, all who call out to Him with integrity. He fulfills the desires of those who fear Him; He hears their cry for help and saves them.

PSALM 145:18-19 HCSB

Surely goodness and mercy shall follow me all the days of my life: and I will dwell in the house of the Lord for ever.

PSALM 23:6 KJV

I am not alone, because the Father is with Me.

JOHN 16:32 HCSB

I have set the Lord always before me; because He is at my right hand I shall not be moved.

PSALM 16:8 NKJV

MORE GOOD IDEAS

We need never shout across the spaces to an absent God. He is nearer than our own soul, closer than our most secret thoughts.

A. W. TOZER

There is nothing more important in any life than the constantly enjoyed presence of the Lord. There is nothing more vital, for without it we shall make mistakes, and without it we shall be defeated.

ALAN REDPATH

Let this be your chief object in prayer: to realize the presence of your heavenly Father. Let your watchword be: Alone with God.

ANDREW MURRAY

A TIMELY TIP

If you're here, God is here. If you're there, God is, too. You can't get away from Him or His love . . . thank goodness!

DEAR MOM,
On the Lines Below, Write Down Your Own Ideas About God's Presence

CHAPTER 13

FORGIVENESS NOW

*And whenever you stand praying, if you have anything
against anyone, forgive him, so that your Father in heaven
may also forgive you your wrongdoing.*

—

MARK 11:25 HCSB

Even the most mild-mannered moms will, on occasion,
have reason to become angry with the inevitable
shortcomings of family members and friends. But wise
women are quick to forgive others, just as God has forgiven
them.

Forgiveness is God's commandment, but oh how difficult
a commandment it can be to follow. Being frail, fallible,
imperfect human beings, we are quick to anger, quick to
blame, slow to forgive, and even slower to forget. No matter.
Even when forgiveness is difficult, God's Word is clear.

If, in your heart, you hold bitterness against even a single
person, forgive. If there exists even one person, alive or dead,
whom you have not forgiven, follow God's commandment
and His will for your life: forgive. If you are embittered
against yourself for some past mistake or shortcoming,
forgive. Then, to the best of your abilities, forget, and move
on. Bitterness and regret are not part of God's plan for your
life. Forgiveness is.

MORE GREAT IDEAS ABOUT FORGIVENESS

God expects us to forgive others as He has forgiven us; we are to follow His example by having a forgiving heart.

VONETTE BRIGHT

To be a Christian means to forgive the inexcusable, because God has forgiven the inexcusable in you.

C. S. LEWIS

To hold on to hate and resentments is to throw a monkey wrench into the machinery of life.

E. STANLEY JONES

Forgiveness is actually the best revenge because it not only sets us free from the person we forgive, but it frees us to move into all that God has in store for us.

STORMIE OMARTIAN

Forgiveness is contagious. First you forgive them, and pretty soon, they'll forgive you, too.

MARIE T. FREEMAN

I believe that forgiveness can become a continuing cycle: because God forgives us, we're to forgive others; because we forgive others, God forgives us. Scripture presents both parts of the cycle.

SHIRLEY DOBSON

Forgiveness is the key that unlocks the door of resentment and the handcuffs of hate. It is a power that breaks the chains of bitterness and the shackles of selfishness.

CORRIE TEN BOOM

Sometimes, we need a housecleaning of the heart.

CATHERINE MARSHALL

There is no use in talking as if forgiveness were easy. I could say of a certain man, "Have I forgiven him more times than I can count?" For we find that the work of forgiveness has to be done over and over again.

C. S. LEWIS

We cannot be right with God until we are right with one another.

CHARLES SWINDOLL

MORE WISDOM FROM GOD'S WORD

Be merciful, just as your Father also is merciful.

LUKE 6:36 HCSB

All bitterness, anger and wrath, insult and slander must be removed from you, along with all wickedness. And be kind and compassionate to one another, forgiving one another, just as God also forgave you in Christ.

EPHESIANS 4:31-32 HCSB

Then Peter came to Him and said, "Lord, how many times could my brother sin against me and I forgive him? As many as seven times?" "I tell you, not as many as seven," Jesus said to him, "but 70 times seven."

MATTHEW 18:21-22 HCSB

You have heard that it was said, You shall love your neighbor and hate your enemy. But I tell you, love your enemies, and pray for those who persecute you, so that you may be sons of your Father in heaven.

MATTHEW 5:43-45 HCSB

A person's insight gives him patience, and his virtue is to overlook an offense.

PROVERBS 19:11 HCSB

MORE GOOD IDEAS

Forgiveness is every person's deepest need and the greatest quality of being like Jesus.

FRANKLIN GRAHAM

Forgiveness is God's command.

MARTIN LUTHER

How often should you forgive the other person? Only as many times as you want God to forgive you!

MARIE T. FREEMAN

A TIMELY TIP

Face facts: forgiveness can be a very hard thing to do. No matter. God instructs us to forgive others (and to keep forgiving them), period. As a parent, you must explain to your child that forgiving another person—even when it's difficult—is the right thing to do.

DEAR MOM,
On the Lines Below, Write Down Your Own Ideas About Forgiveness

CHAPTER 14

TRUST HIM

Trust in the Lord with all your heart, and do not rely on your own understanding; think about Him in all your ways, and He will guide you on the right paths.

—

PROVERBS 3:5-6 HCSB

Where will you place your trust today? Will you trust in the ways of the world, or will you trust in the Word and the will of your Creator?

If you aspire to do great things for God's kingdom, you will trust Him completely.

Trusting God means trusting Him in every aspect of your life. You must trust Him with your relationships. You must trust Him with your finances. You must follow His commandments and pray for His guidance. Then, you can wait patiently for God's revelations and for His blessings.

When you trust your Heavenly Father without reservation, you can rest assured: in His own fashion and in His own time, God will bless you in ways that you never could have imagined. So trust Him, and then prepare yourself for the abundance and joy that will most certainly be yours through Him.

MORE GREAT IDEAS ABOUT TRUSTING GOD

Do not be afraid, then, that if you trust, or tell others to trust, the matter will end there. Trust is only the beginning and the continual foundation. When we trust Him, the Lord works, and His work is the important part of the whole matter.

HANNAH WHITALL SMITH

Brother, is your faith looking upward today? / Trust in the promise of the Savior. / Sister, is the light shining bright on your way? / Trust in the promise of thy Lord.

FANNY CROSBY

Sometimes the very essence of faith is trusting God in the midst of things He knows good and well we cannot comprehend.

BETH MOORE

Are you serious about wanting God's guidance to become the person he wants you to be? The first step is to tell God that you know you can't manage your own life; that you need his help.

CATHERINE MARSHALL

Never be afraid to trust an unknown future to a known God.

CORRIE TEN BOOM

As God's children, we are the recipients of lavish love—a love that motivates us to keep trusting even when we have no idea what God is doing.

BETH MOORE

Once we recognize our need for Jesus, then the building of our faith begins. It is a daily, moment-by-moment life of absolute dependence upon Him for everything.

CATHERINE MARSHALL

When the train goes through a tunnel and the world becomes dark, do you jump out? Of course not. You sit still and trust the engineer to get you through.

CORRIE TEN BOOM

The Rock of Ages is the great sheltering encirclement.

OSWALD CHAMBERS

MORE WISDOM FROM GOD'S WORD

For the eyes of the Lord range throughout the earth to show Himself strong for those whose hearts are completely His.

2 CHRONICLES 16:9 HCSB

He granted their request because they trusted in Him.

1 CHRONICLES 5:20 HCSB

Let us hold fast the confession of our hope without wavering, for He who promised is faithful.

HEBREWS 10:23 NKJV

The one who understands a matter finds success, and the one who trusts in the Lord will be happy.

PROVERBS 16:20 HCSB

I know whom I have believed and am persuaded that He is able to guard what has been entrusted to me until that day.

2 TIMOTHY 1:12 HCSB

God's Protection

Have you ever faced challenges that seemed too big to handle? Have you ever faced big problems that, despite your best efforts, simply could not be solved? If so, you know how uncomfortable it is to feel helpless in the face of difficult circumstances. Thankfully, even when there's nowhere else to turn, you can turn your thoughts and prayers to God, and He will respond.

God's hand uplifts those who turn their hearts and prayers to Him. Count yourself among that number. When you do, you can live courageously and joyfully, knowing that "this too will pass"—but that God's love for you will not. And you can draw strength from the knowledge that you are a marvelous creation, loved, protected, and uplifted by the ever-present hand of God.

MORE GOOD IDEAS

Faith is not merely you holding on to God—it is God holding on to you.

E. STANLEY JONES

The last and greatest lesson that the soul has to learn is the fact that God, and God alone, is enough for all its needs. This is the lesson that all His dealings with us are meant to teach; and this is the crowning discovery of our whole Christian life. God is enough!

HANNAH WHITALL SMITH

Only God can move mountains, but faith and prayer can move God.

E. M. BOUNDS

A TIMELY TIP

One of the most important lessons that you can ever learn is to trust God for everything, and that includes timing . . . In other words, you should trust God to decide the best time for things to happen. Sometimes it's hard to trust God, but it's always the right thing to do.

DEAR MOM,
On the Lines Below, Write Down Your Own Ideas About Trusting God

AND FINALLY . . .

IF GOD IS YOUR CO-PILOT . . . SWAP SEATS!

CHAPTER 15

THE POWER OF PATIENCE

Rejoice in hope; be patient in affliction;
be persistent in prayer.

—

ROMANS 12:12 HCSB

The rigors of motherhood can test the patience of the most even-tempered moms: From time to time, even the most mannerly children may do things that worry us or confuse us or anger us. Why? Because they are children, and because they are human.

As loving parents, we must be patient with our children's shortcomings (just as they, too, must be patient with our own). But our patience must not be restricted to those who live under our care. We must also strive, to the best of our abilities, to exercise patience in all our dealings, because our children are watching and learning.

Sometimes, patience is simply the price we pay for being responsible parents, and that's exactly as it should be. After all, think how patient our Heavenly Father has been with us.

MORE GREAT IDEAS ABOUT
PATIENCE

Let me encourage you to continue to wait with faith. God may not perform a miracle, but He is trustworthy to touch you and make you whole where there used to be a hole.

LISA WHELCHEL

Waiting is the hardest kind of work, but God knows best, and we may joyfully leave all in His hands.

LOTTIE MOON

We must learn to wait. There is grace supplied to the one who waits.

MRS. CHARLES E. COWMAN

How do you wait upon the Lord? First you must learn to sit at His feet and take time to listen to His words.

KAY ARTHUR

When we read of the great Biblical leaders, we see that it was not uncommon for God to ask them to wait, not just a day or two, but for years, until God was ready for them to act.

GLORIA GAITHER

Be patient. God is using today's difficulties to strengthen you for tomorrow. He is equipping you. The God who makes things grow will help you bear fruit.

MAX LUCADO

Waiting is an essential part of spiritual discipline. It can be the ultimate test of faith.

ANNE GRAHAM LOTZ

God is in no hurry. Compared to the works of mankind, He is extremely deliberate. God is not a slave to the human clock.

CHARLES SWINDOLL

Those who have had to wait and work for happiness seem to enjoy it more, because they never take it for granted.

BARBARA JOHNSON

If you want to hear God's voice clearly and you are uncertain, then remain in His presence until He changes that uncertainty. Often much can happen during this waiting for the Lord. Sometimes he changes pride into humility; doubt into faith and peace . . . .

CORRIE TEN BOOM

MORE WISDOM FROM GOD'S WORD

Love is patient; love is kind.

1 CORINTHIANS 13:4 HCSB

A patient spirit is better than a proud spirit.

ECCLESIASTES 7:8 HCSB

Therefore the Lord is waiting to show you mercy, and is rising up to show you compassion, for the Lord is a just God. Happy are all who wait patiently for Him.

ISAIAH 30:18 HCSB

Be gentle to everyone, able to teach, and patient.

2 TIMOTHY 2:23 HCSB

My brethren, count it all joy when you fall into various trials, knowing that the testing of your faith produces patience. But let patience have its perfect work, that you may be perfect and complete, lacking nothing.

JAMES 1:2-4 NKJV

TRUST GOD'S TIMING

If you're in a hurry for good things to happen to you and your family, you're not the only mom on the block who feels that way. But sometimes, you'll simply have to be patient.

God has created a world that unfolds according to His own timetable, not ours . . . thank goodness! We mortals might make a terrible mess of things. God does not.

Of course, God's plans do not always unfold according to our own wishes, or at the time of our own choosing. Nonetheless, we should trust the benevolent, all-knowing Father as we wait patiently for Him to reveal Himself. Until God's plans are made clear to us, we must walk in faith and never lose hope, knowing that His plans are always best. Always.

MORE GOOD IDEAS

When our plans are interrupted, his are not. His plans are proceeding exactly as scheduled, moving us always—including those minutes or hours or years which seem most useless or wasted or unendurable—toward the goal of true maturity.

ELISABETH ELLIOT

Your times are in His hands. He's in charge of the timetable, so wait patiently.

KAY ARTHUR

God's delays and His ways can be confusing because the process God uses to accomplish His will can go against human logic and common sense.

ANNE GRAHAM LOTZ

A TIMELY TIP

Be patient with your child's impatience. Children are supposed to be more impulsive than adults; after all, they're still kids. So be understanding of your child's limitations and understanding of his or her imperfections.

DEAR MOM,
On the Lines Below, Write Down Your Own Ideas About
The Power of Patience

And Finally . . .

A mother's patience
is like a tube of toothpaste:
It's never quite gone.

CHAPTER 16

CONTINUING TO GROW

*For this reason also, since the day we heard this,
we haven't stopped praying for you.
We are asking that you may be filled with the knowledge
of His will in all wisdom and spiritual understanding.*

—

COLOSSIANS 1:9 HCSB

The journey toward spiritual maturity lasts a lifetime: As Christian mothers, we can and should continue to grow in the love and the knowledge of our Savior as long as we live. When we cease to grow, either emotionally or spiritually, we do ourselves and our loved ones a profound disservice. But, if we study God's Word, if we obey His commandments, and if we live in the center of His will, we will not be "stagnant" believers; we will, instead, be growing Christians . . . and that's exactly what God wants for our lives.

Many of life's most important lessons are painful to learn. During times of heartbreak and hardship, God stands ready to protect us. As Psalm 147 promises, "He heals the brokenhearted and bandages their wounds" (NCV). In His own time and according to His master plan, God will heal us if we invite Him into our hearts.

Spiritual growth need not take place only in times of adversity. We should seek to grow in our relationship with the Lord through every season of our lives, through happy times and hard times, through times of celebration and times of pain.

In those quiet moments when we open our hearts to God, the One who made us keeps remaking us. He gives us direction, perspective, wisdom, and courage. And of course, the appropriate moment to accept those spiritual gifts is always the present one.

MORE GREAT IDEAS ABOUT SPIRITUAL GROWTH

If all struggles and sufferings were eliminated, the spirit would no more reach maturity than would the child.

ELISABETH ELLIOT

We look at our burdens and heavy loads, and we shrink from them. But, if we lift them and bind them about our hearts, they become wings, and on them we can rise and soar toward God.

MRS. CHARLES E. COWMAN

We set our eyes on the finish line, forgetting the past, and straining toward the mark of spiritual maturity and fruitfulness.

VONETTE BRIGHT

Grow, dear friends, but grow, I beseech you, in God's way, which is the only true way.

HANNAH WHITALL SMITH

You are either becoming more like Christ every day or you're becoming less like Him. There is no neutral position in the Lord.

STORMIE OMARTIAN

Growth in depth and strength and consistency and fruitfulness and ultimately in Christlikeness is only possible when the winds of life are contrary to personal comfort.

ANNE GRAHAM LOTZ

God is teaching me to become more and more "teachable": To keep evolving. To keep taking the risk of learning something new . . . or unlearning something old and off base.

BETH MOORE

MORE WISDOM FROM GOD'S WORD

But grow in the grace and knowledge of our Lord and Savior Jesus Christ. To Him be the glory both now and to the day of eternity.

2 PETER 3:18 HCSB

I want their hearts to be encouraged and joined together in love, so that they may have all the riches of assured understanding, and have the knowledge of God's mystery—Christ.

COLOSSIANS 2:2 HCSB

For You, O God, have tested us; You have refined us as silver is refined. You brought us into the net; You laid affliction on our backs. You have caused men to ride over our heads; we went through fire and through water; but You brought us out to rich fulfillment.

PSALM 66:10–12 NKJV

For though by this time you ought to be teachers, you need someone to teach you again the basic principles of God's revelation. You need milk, not solid food. Now everyone who lives on milk is inexperienced with the message about righteousness, because he is an infant. But solid food is for the mature—for those whose senses have been trained to distinguish between good and evil.

HEBREWS 5:12-14 HCSB

MORE GOOD IDEAS

Salvation is the process that's done, that's secure, that no one can take away from you. Sanctification is the lifelong process of being changed from one degree of glory to the next, growing in Christ, putting away the old, taking on the new.

MAX LUCADO

Spiritual growth consists most in the growth of the root, which is out of sight.

MATTHEW HENRY

A Christian is never in a state of completion but always in the process of becoming.

MARTIN LUTHER

A TIMELY TIP

Spiritual maturity is a journey, not a destination. A growing relationship with God should be your highest priority.

DEAR MOM,
On the Lines Below, Write Down Your Own Ideas About Spiritual Growth

CHAPTER 17

THIS IS THE DAY

This is the day the LORD has made;
we will rejoice and be glad in it.

—

PSALM 118:24 NKJV

The 100th Psalm reminds us that the entire earth should "Shout for joy to the Lord" (NIV). As God's children, we are blessed beyond measure, but sometimes, as busy mothers living in a demanding world, we are slow to count our gifts and even slower to give thanks to the Giver.

Our blessings include faith, life, and family—for starters. And, the gifts we receive from God are multiplied when we share them. May we always give thanks to the Creator for His blessings, and may we always demonstrate our gratitude by sharing our gifts with others.

The 118th Psalm reminds us that, "This is the day which the LORD has made; let us rejoice and be glad in it" (v. 24, NASB). May we celebrate this day and the One who created it.

MORE GREAT IDEAS ABOUT TODAY

If you can forgive the person you were, accept the person you are, and believe in the person you will become, you are headed for joy. So celebrate your life.

BARBARA JOHNSON

Yesterday is the tomb of time, and tomorrow is the womb of time. Only now is yours.

R. G. LEE

Christ is the secret, the source, the substance, the center, and the circumference of all true and lasting gladness.

MRS. CHARLES E. COWMAN

If we are ever going to be or do anything for our Lord, now is the time.

VANCE HAVNER

Jesus intended for us to be overwhelmed by the blessings of regular days. He said it was the reason he had come: "I am come that they might have life, and that they might have it more abundantly."

GLORIA GAITHER

When the dream of our heart is one that God has planted there, a strange happiness flows into us. At that moment, all of the spiritual resources of the universe are released to help us. Our praying is then at one with the will of God and becomes a channel for the Creator's purposes for us and our world.

CATHERINE MARSHALL

God gave you this glorious day. Don't disappoint Him. Use it for His glory.

MARIE T. FREEMAN

Submit each day to God, knowing that He is God over all your tomorrows.

KAY ARTHUR

Love, joy, peace, patience, kindness, goodness, faithfulness, gentleness, and self-control. To these I commit my day. If I succeed, I will give thanks. If I fail, I will seek his grace. And then, when this day is done, I will place my head on my pillow and rest.

MAX LUCADO

MORE WISDOM FROM GOD'S WORD

Working together with Him, we also appeal to you: "Don't receive God's grace in vain." For He says: In an acceptable time, I heard you, and in the day of salvation, I helped you. Look, now is the acceptable time; look, now is the day of salvation.

2 CORINTHIANS 6:1-2 HCSB

I must work the works of Him who sent Me while it is day; the night is coming when no one can work.

JOHN 9:4 NKJV

Therefore, get your minds ready for action, being self-disciplined, and set your hope completely on the grace to be brought to you at the revelation of Jesus Christ.

1 PETER 1:13 HCSB

Rejoice in the Lord always. I will say it again: Rejoice!

PHILIPPIANS 4:4 HCSB

But encourage each other daily, while it is still called today, so that none of you is hardened by sin's deception.

HEBREWS 3:13 HCSB

MORE GOOD IDEAS

People create success in their lives by focusing on today. It may sound trite, but today is the only time you have. It's too late for yesterday. And you can't depend on tomorrow.

JOHN MAXWELL

When your life comes to a close, you will remember not days but moments. Treasure each one.

BARBARA JOHNSON

With each new dawn, life delivers a package to your front door, rings your doorbell, and runs.

CHARLES SWINDOLL

A TIMELY TIP

If you don't feel like celebrating today, start counting your blessings. Before long, you'll realize that you have plenty of reasons to celebrate.

DEAR MOM,
On the Lines Below, Write Down Your Own Ideas About
The Need to Celebrate Each Day

CHAPTER 18

MAINTAINING PERSPECTIVE

Make your own attitude that of Christ Jesus.

—

PHILIPPIANS 2:5 HCSB

E ven if you're the world's most thoughtful mom, you may, from time to time, lose perspective—it happens on those days when life seems out of balance and the pressures of motherhood seem overwhelming. What's needed is a fresh perspective, a restored sense of balance… and God.

If a temporary loss of perspective has left you worried, exhausted, or both, it's time to readjust your thought patterns. Negative thoughts are habit-forming; thankfully, so are positive ones. With practice, you can form the habit of focusing on God's priorities and your possibilities. When you do, you'll spend less time fretting about your challenges and more time praising God for His gifts.

So today and every day hereafter, pray for a sense of balance and perspective. And remember: your thoughts are intensely powerful things, so handle them with care.

MORE GREAT IDEAS ABOUT PERSPECTIVE

Attitude is the mind's paintbrush; it can color any situation.

BARBARA JOHNSON

Like a shadow declining swiftly . . . away . . . like the dew of the morning gone with the heat of the day; like the wind in the treetops, like a wave of the sea, so are our lives on earth when seen in light of eternity.

RUTH BELL GRAHAM

Instead of being frustrated and overwhelmed by all that is going on in our world, go to the Lord and ask Him to give you His eternal perspective.

KAY ARTHUR

The proper perspective creates within us a spirit of reaching outside of ourselves with joy and enthusiasm.

LUCI SWINDOLL

What you see and hear depends a good deal on where you are standing; it also depends on what sort of person you are.

C. S. LEWIS

Joy is the direct result of having God's perspective on our daily lives and the effect of loving our Lord enough to obey His commands and trust His promises.

BILL BRIGHT

Obey God one step at a time, then the next step will come into view.

CATHERINE MARSHALL

When you and I hurt deeply, what we really need is not an explanation from God but a revelation of God. We need to see how great God is; we need to recover our lost perspective on life. Things get out of proportion when we are suffering, and it takes a vision of something bigger than ourselves to get life's dimensions adjusted again.

WARREN WIERSBE

Earthly fears are no fears at all. Answer the big questions of eternity, and the little questions of life fall into perspective.

MAX LUCADO

MORE WISDOM FROM GOD'S WORD

Finally brothers, whatever is true, whatever is honorable, whatever is just, whatever is pure, whatever is lovely, whatever is commendable—if there is any moral excellence and if there is any praise—dwell on these things.

PHILIPPIANS 4:8 HCSB

Set your minds on what is above, not on what is on the earth.

COLOSSIANS 3:2 HCSB

Let this mind be in you which was also in Christ Jesus, who, being in the form of God, did not consider it robbery to be equal with God, but made Himself of no reputation, taking the form of a bondservant, and coming in the likeness of men. And being found in appearance as a man, He humbled Himself and became obedient to the point of death, even the death of the cross.

PHILIPPIANS 2:5-8 NKJV

For the word of God is living and powerful, and sharper than any two-edged sword, piercing even to the division of soul and spirit, and of joints and marrow, and is a discerner of the thoughts and intents of the heart.

HEBREWS 4:12 NKJV

No More Mental Garbage

Mental garbage has a way of gradually building up in the minds of even the most optimistic moms, so you should keep yourself on guard against that messy collection of negative thoughts, wrongheaded ideas, irrational notions, and unhelpful ruminations that can, at times, swirl around in your brain. Those kinds of thoughts have the power to turn your mind into the psychological equivalent of a landfill.

When you feel that your healthy thoughts have morphed into sloppy thinking, it's time to take out the garbage by talking to someone you can trust and by talking to God. When you do, you'll start recycling those bad thoughts and turning them into good ones.

So the next time your thoughts migrate toward the negative end of the spectrum, do the healthy thing: open up your mind . . . and take out the trash.

MORE GOOD IDEAS

Every major spiritual battle is in the mind.

CHARLES STANLEY

No matter how little we can change about our circumstances, we always have a choice about our attitude toward the situation.

VONETTE BRIGHT

Winners see an answer for every problem; losers see a problem in every answer.

BARBARA JOHNSON

A TIMELY TIP

Keep things in perspective. Your life is an integral part of God's grand plan. So don't become unduly upset over the minor inconveniences of life, and don't worry too much about today's setbacks—they're temporary.

DEAR MOM,
On the Lines Below, Write Down Your Own Ideas About
Keeping Things in Perspective

And Finally . . .

Did You Know?

In the United States, August is the most popular month to have a baby.

CHAPTER 19

ACCEPTING GOD'S ABUNDANCE

I am come that they might have life,
and that they might have it more abundantly.

—

JOHN 10:10 KJV

D o you seek God's abundance for yourself and your family? Of course you do. And it's worth remembering that God's rewards are most certainly available to you and yours. The 10th chapter of John tells us that Christ came to earth so that our lives might be filled with abundance. But what, exactly, did Jesus mean when He promised "life . . . more abundantly"? Was He referring to material possessions or financial wealth? Hardly. Jesus offers a different kind of abundance: a spiritual richness that extends beyond the temporal boundaries of this world. This everlasting abundance is available to all who seek it and claim it. May you and your family claim those riches, and may you share Christ's blessings with all who cross your path.

MORE GREAT IDEAS ABOUT ABUNDANCE

The gift of God is eternal life, spiritual life, abundant life through faith in Jesus Christ, the Living Word of God.

ANNE GRAHAM LOTZ

Yes, we were created for His holy pleasure, but we will ultimately—if not immediately—find much pleasure in His pleasure.

BETH MOORE

It would be wrong to have a "poverty complex," for to think ourselves paupers is to deny either the King's riches or to deny our being His children.

CATHERINE MARSHALL

Jesus intended for us to be overwhelmed by the blessings of regular days. He said it was the reason he had come: "I am come that they might have life, and that they might have it more abundantly."

GLORIA GAITHER

Jesus wants Life for us, Life with a capital L.

JOHN ELDREDGE

God has promised us abundance, peace, and eternal life. These treasures are ours for the asking; all we must do is claim them. One of the great mysteries of life is why on earth do so many of us wait so very long to lay claim to God's gifts?

MARIE T. FREEMAN

Get ready for God to show you not only His pleasure, but His approval.

JONI EARECKSON TADA

God is the giver, and we are the receivers. And His richest gifts are bestowed not upon those who do the greatest things, but upon those who accept His abundance and His grace.

HANNAH WHITALL SMITH

God's riches are beyond anything we could ask or even dare to imagine! If my life gets gooey and stale, I have no excuse.

BARBARA JOHNSON

God loves you and wants you to experience peace and life— abundant and eternal.

BILLY GRAHAM

MORE WISDOM FROM GOD'S WORD

Until now you have asked for nothing in My name. Ask and you will receive, that your joy may be complete.

JOHN 16:24 HCSB

And God is able to make every grace overflow to you, so that in every way, always having everything you need, you may excel in every good work.

2 CORINTHIANS 9:8 HCSB

My cup runs over. Surely goodness and mercy shall follow me all the days of my life; and I will dwell in the house of the Lord forever.

PSALM 23:5-6 NKJV

Come to terms with God and be at peace; in this way good will come to you.

JOB 22:21 HCSB

And He said to them, "Take heed and beware of covetousness, for one's life does not consist in the abundance of the things he possesses."

LUKE 12:15 NKJV

DREAM BIG

It takes courage to dream big dreams—dreams for yourself and your family. You'll discover the courage to dream big when you do three things: accept the past, trust God to handle the future, and make the most of the time He has given you today.

Are you excited about the opportunities of today and thrilled by the possibilities of tomorrow? Do you confidently expect God to lead you and yours to a place of abundance, peace, and joy? If you trust God's promises, you should believe that your future is intensely and eternally bright.

Today, promise yourself that you'll do your family (and the world) a king-sized favor by whole-heartedly pursuing your dreams. After all, no dreams are too big for God—not even yours. So start living—and dreaming—accordingly.

MORE GOOD IDEAS

Allow your dreams a place in your prayers and plans. God-given dreams can help you move into the future He is preparing for you.

BARBARA JOHNSON

Set goals so big that unless God helps you, you will be a miserable failure.

BILL BRIGHT

You cannot out-dream God.

JOHN ELDREDGE

A TIMELY TIP

If you're having tough times, don't hit the panic button and don't keep everything bottled up inside. Talk things over with people you can really trust. And if your troubles seem overwhelming, be willing to seek help—starting, of course, with your spouse and your pastor.

DEAR MOM,
On the Lines Below, Write Down Your Own Ideas About Lessons You've Learned from Tough Times

AND FINALLY . . .

Wealth is not his that has it,
but his that enjoys it.

—

POOR RICHARD'S ALMANAC

CHAPTER 20

THANKSGIVING NOW

In everything give thanks;
for this is the will of God in Christ Jesus for you.

—

1 THESSALONIANS 5:18 NKJV

As believing Christians, we are blessed beyond measure. God sent His only Son to die for our sins. And, God has given us the priceless gifts of eternal love and eternal life. We, in turn, are instructed to approach our Heavenly Father with reverence and thanksgiving. But, as busy mothers caught up in the inevitable demands of everyday life, we sometimes fail to pause and thank our Creator for the countless blessings He has bestowed upon us.

When we slow down and express our gratitude to the One who made us, we enrich our own lives and the lives of our loved ones. Thanksgiving should become a habit, a regular part of our daily routines. Yes, God has blessed us beyond measure, and we owe Him everything, including our eternal praise.

MORE GREAT IDEAS ABOUT THANKSGIVING

God is worthy of our praise and is pleased when we come before Him with thanksgiving.

SHIRLEY DOBSON

The act of thanksgiving is a demonstration of the fact that you are going to trust and believe God.

KAY ARTHUR

Thanksgiving is good but Thanksliving is better.

JIM GALLERY

Thanksgiving or complaining—these words express two contrastive attitudes of the souls of God's children in regard to His dealings with them. The soul that gives thanks can find comfort in everything; the soul that complains can find comfort in nothing.

HANNAH WHITALL SMITH

It is always possible to be thankful for what is given rather than to complain about what is not given. One or the other becomes a habit of life.

ELISABETH ELLIOT

Do you know that if at birth I had been able to make one petition, it would have been that I should be born blind? Because, when I get to heaven, the first face that shall ever gladden my sight will be that of my Savior!

FANNY CROSBY

Words fail to express my love for this holy Book, my gratitude for its author, for His love and goodness. How shall I thank him for it?

LOTTIE MOON

If you pause to think—you'll have cause to thank!

ANONYMOUS

A child of God should be a visible beatitude for joy and a living doxology for gratitude.

C. H. SPURGEON

The words "thank" and "think" come from the same root word. If we would think more, we would thank more.

WARREN WIERSBE

MORE WISDOM FROM GOD'S WORD

Thanks be to God for His indescribable gift.

2 CORINTHIANS 9:15 HCSB

Therefore as you have received Christ Jesus the Lord, walk in Him, rooted and built up in Him and established in the faith, just as you were taught, and overflowing with thankfulness.

COLOSSIANS 2:6-7 HCSB

Enter into His gates with thanksgiving, and into His courts with praise. Be thankful to Him, and bless His name. For the Lord is good; His mercy is everlasting, and His truth endures to all generations.

PSALM 100:4-5 NKJV

And whatever you do, in word or in deed, do everything in the name of the Lord Jesus, giving thanks to God the Father through Him.

COLOSSIANS 3:17 HCSB

Give thanks to the Lord, for He is good; His faithful love endures forever.

PSALM 106:1 HCSB

WORSHIP HIM!

God has a wonderful plan for your life, and an important part of that plan includes worship. We should never deceive ourselves: every life is based upon some form of worship. The question is not whether we worship, but what we worship.

Some of us choose to worship God. The result is a plentiful harvest of joy, peace, and abundance. Others distance themselves from God by foolishly worshiping earthly possessions and personal gratification. To do so is a mistake of profound proportions.

Have you accepted the grace of God's only begotten Son? Then worship Him and thank Him today and every day. Worship Him with sincerity and thanksgiving. Write His name on your heart and rest assured that He, too, has written your name on His.

MORE GOOD IDEAS

In the sanctuary, we discover beauty: the beauty of His presence.

KAY ARTHUR

God asks that we worship Him with our concentrated minds as well as with our wills and emotions. A divided and scattered mind is not effective.

CATHERINE MARSHALL

Spiritual worship comes from our very core and is fueled by an awesome reverence and desire for God.

BETH MOORE

A TIMELY TIP

As the parent, you have an important task: deciding when and how your family will worship and thank God. You should weave genuine worship and praise into the fabric of family life by honoring God sincerely and often (not just on Sunday mornings).

DEAR MOM,
On the Lines Below, Write Down Your Own Ideas About
Things to Be Thankful For

AND FINALLY . . .

OF ALL THE THINGS YOU WEAR,
YOUR EXPRESSION
IS THE MOST IMPORTANT.

CHAPTER 21

YOUR JOURNEY
WITH GOD

*For it is God who is working among you
both the willing and the working for His good purpose.*

—

PHILIPPIANS 2:13 HCSB

Life is best lived on purpose, not by accident: the sooner we discover what God intends for us to do with our lives, the better. But God's purposes aren't always clear to us. Sometimes, the responsibilities of caring for our loved ones leave us precious little time to discern God's will for ourselves. At other times, we may struggle mightily against God in a vain effort to find success and happiness through our own means, not His.

Whenever we struggle against God's plans, we suffer. When we resist God's calling, our efforts bear little fruit. Our best strategy, therefore, is to seek God's wisdom and follow Him wherever He chooses to lead. When we do so, we are blessed.

As a loving mother, you know intuitively that God has important plans for you and your family. But how can you know precisely what God's intentions are? The answer, of course, is that even the most well-intentioned believers face periods of uncertainty about the direction of their lives. So, too, will you.

When you arrive at one of life's inevitable crossroads, that is precisely the moment when you should turn your thoughts and prayers toward God. When you do, He will make Himself known to you in a time and manner of His choosing.

Are you earnestly seeking to discern God's purpose for your life? If so, these pages are intended as a reminder of several important facts: 1. God has a plan for your life; 2. If you seek that plan sincerely and prayerfully, you will find it; 3. When you discover God's purpose for your life, you will experience abundance, peace, joy, and power—God's power. And that's the only kind of power that really matters.

His life is our light—
our purpose and meaning and reason for living.

—

ANNE GRAHAM LOTZ

MORE GREAT IDEAS ABOUT
PURPOSE

Only God's chosen task for you will ultimately satisfy. Do not wait until it is too late to realize the privilege of serving Him in His chosen position for you.

BETH MOORE

In the very place where God has put us, whatever its limitations, whatever kind of work it may be, we may indeed serve the Lord Christ.

ELISABETH ELLIOT

How much of our lives are, well, so daily. How often our hours are filled with the mundane, seemingly unimportant things that have to be done, whether at home or work. These very "daily" tasks could become a celebration of praise. "It is through consecration," someone has said, "that drudgery is made divine."

GIGI GRAHAM TCHIVIDJIAN

If you want purpose and meaning and satisfaction and fulfillment and peace and hope and joy and abundant life that lasts forever, look to Jesus.

ANNE GRAHAM LOTZ

MORE WISDOM FROM GOD'S WORD

We know that all things work together for the good of those who love God: those who are called according to His purpose.

ROMANS 8:28 HCSB

I will instruct you and show you the way to go; with My eye on you, I will give counsel.

PSALM 32:8 HCSB

You reveal the path of life to me; in Your presence is abundant joy; in Your right hand are eternal pleasures.

PSALM 16:11 HCSB

Commit your activities to the Lord and your plans will be achieved.

PROVERBS 16:3 HCSB

To everything there is a season, a time for every purpose under heaven.

ECCLESIASTES 3:1 NKJV

MORE GOOD IDEAS

Sometimes the very essence of faith is trusting God in the midst of things He knows good and well we cannot comprehend.

BETH MOORE

Are you serious about wanting God's guidance to become the person he wants you to be? The first step is to tell God that you know you can't manage your own life; that you need his help.

CATHERINE MARSHALL

Blessed are those who know what on earth they are here on earth to do and set themselves about the business of doing it.

MAX LUCADO

A TIMELY TIP

God has a wonderful plan for your life. And the time to start looking for that plan—and living it—is now. (Psalm 16:11)

DEAR MOM,
On the Lines Below, Write Down Your Own Ideas About Living on Purpose

CHAPTER 22

HE WANTS YOU
TO SERVE

Worship the Lord your God and . . . serve Him only.

—

MATTHEW 4:10 HCSB

I f you genuinely seek to discover God's unfolding purpose for your life, you must ask yourself this question: "How does God want me to serve my family and my community today?"

Whatever your path, whatever your career, whatever your calling, you may be certain of this: service to others is an integral part of God's plan for your life.

Every single day of your life, including this one, God will give you opportunities to serve Him by serving His children. Welcome those opportunities with open arms. They are God's gift to you, His way of allowing you to achieve greatness in His kingdom. And of this you can be certain: God wants you to serve early and often, and He will surely reward you for your willingness to share your talents and your time with your family and the world.

MORE GREAT IDEAS ABOUT SERVICE

God wants us to serve Him with a willing spirit, one that would choose no other way.

BETH MOORE

Through our service to others, God wants to influence our world for Him.

VONETTE BRIGHT

In the very place where God has put us, whatever its limitations, whatever kind of work it may be, we may indeed serve the Lord Christ.

ELISABETH ELLIOT

Doing something positive toward another person is a practical approach to feeling good about yourself.

BARBARA JOHNSON

If you want to discover your spiritual gifts, start obeying God. As you serve Him, you will find that He has given you the gifts that are necessary to follow through in obedience.

ANNE GRAHAM LOTZ

So many times we say that we can't serve God because we aren't whatever is needed. We're not talented enough or smart enough or whatever. But if you are in covenant with Jesus Christ, He is responsible for covering your weaknesses, for being your strength. He will give you His abilities for your disabilities!

KAY ARTHUR

God has lots of folks who intend to go to work for him "some day." What He needs is more people who are willing to work for Him today.

MARIE T. FREEMAN

Jesus never asks us to give Him what we don't have. But He does demand that we give Him all we do have if we want to be a part of what He wishes to do in the lives of those around us!

ANNE GRAHAM LOTZ

Opportunities for service abound, and you will be surprised that when you seek God's direction, a place of suitable service will emerge where you can express your love through service.

CHARLES STANLEY

MORE WISDOM FROM GOD'S WORD

A person should consider us in this way: as servants of Christ and managers of God's mysteries. In this regard, it is expected of managers that each one be found faithful.

1 CORINTHIANS 4:1-2 HCSB

If they serve Him obediently, they will end their days in prosperity and their years in happiness.

JOB 36:11 HCSB

We must do the works of Him who sent Me while it is day. Night is coming when no one can work.

JOHN 9:4 HCSB

Serve the Lord with gladness.

PSALM 100:2 HCSB

If anyone serves Me, let him follow Me; and where I am, there My servant will be also. If anyone serves Me, him My Father will honor.

JOHN 12:26 NKJV

MORE GOOD IDEAS

If the attitude of servanthood is learned, by attending to God as Lord, then serving others will develop as a very natural way of life.

EUGENE PETERSON

We can love Jesus in the hungry, the naked, and the destitute who are dying . . . . If you love, you will be willing to serve. And you will find Jesus in the distressing disguise of the poor.

MOTHER TERESA

In the great orchestra we call life, you have an instrument and a song, and you owe it to God to play them both sublimely.

MAX LUCADO

A TIMELY TIP

Jesus was a servant, and if you want to follow Him, you must be a servant, too—even when service requires sacrifice.

DEAR MOM,
On the Lines Below, Write Down Your Own Ideas About
The Need to Serve

CHAPTER 23

GOD'S GIFT TO YOU: YOUR CHILDREN

Train up a child in the way he should go,
and when he is old he will not depart from it.

—

PROVERBS 22:6 NKJV

As a mother, you are keenly aware that God has entrusted you with a priceless treasure from above: your child. Every child is different, yet every child is similar in this respect: every child is a glorious gift from above—and with that gift comes immense responsibilities.

Thoughtful mothers (like you) understand the critical importance of raising their children with love, with family, with discipline, and with God. By making God a focus in the home, loving mothers offer a priceless legacy to their children—a legacy of hope, a legacy of love, a legacy of wisdom.

Today, let us pray for our children . . . all of them. Let us pray for our own children and for children around the world. Every child is God's child. May we, as concerned mothers, behave—and pray—accordingly.

MORE GREAT IDEAS ABOUT CHILDREN

Children are not casual guests in our home. They have been loaned to us temporarily for the purpose of loving them and instilling a foundation of values on which their future lives will be built.

JAMES DOBSON

Praying for our children is a noble task. There is nothing more special, more precious, than time that a parent spends struggling and pondering with God on behalf of a child.

MAX LUCADO

The balance of affirmation and discipline, freedom and restraint, encouragement and warning is different for each child and season and generation, yet the absolutes of God's Word are necessary and trustworthy at all times.

GLORIA GAITHER

The only real qualifications that parents need is a sincere and diligent desire to follow God's ways. God knew your strengths and weaknesses when you signed up to be a parent, and He still hired you.

LISA WHELCHEL

If you want a surefire way to reshape the future, here it is: find something important to say to the next generation . . . and say it.

MARIE T. FREEMAN

Our faithfulness, or lack of it, will have an overwhelming impact on the heritage of our children.

BETH MOORE

Children are not so different from kites. Children were created to fly. But, they need wind, the undergirding, and strength that comes from unconditional love, encouragement, and prayer.

GIGI GRAHAM TCHIVIDJIAN

Pray over your children and touch them even as they go out the door to school. You will be giving them a blessing for the day.

CHARLES SWINDOLL

The children taught me much as they were growing up: about themselves, about the world around them, about me, and especially about God.

RUTH BELL GRAHAM

MORE WISDOM FROM GOD'S WORD

Teach them to your children, talking about them when you sit in your house and when you walk along the road, when you lie down and when you get up. Write them on the doorposts of your house and on your gates, so that as long as the heavens are above the earth, your days and those of your children may be many in the land the Lord swore to give your fathers.

DEUTERONOMY 11:19-21 HCSB

I have no greater joy than this: to hear that my children are walking in the truth.

3 JOHN 1:4 HCSB

For the promise is for you and for your children.

ACTS 2:39 HCSB

I assure you: Whoever does not welcome the kingdom of God like a little child will never enter it.

LUKE 18:17 HCSB

Listen, my son, to your father's instruction, and don't reject your mother's teaching.

PROVERBS 1:8 HCSB

A MOTHER'S LOVE

There are times when only a Mother's love
Can understand our tears,
Can soothe our disappoints
And calm all of our fears.

There are times when only a Mother's love
Can share the joy we feel
When something we've dreamed about
Quite suddenly is real.

There are times when only a Mother's faith
Can help us on life's way
And inspire in us the confidence
We need from day to day.

For a Mother's heart and a Mother's faith
And a Mother's steadfast love
Were fashioned by the Angels
And sent from God above . . .

AUTHOR UNKNOWN

MORE GOOD IDEAS

Every child born into the world is a new thought of God, an ever-fresh and radiant possibility.

KATE DOUGLAS WIGGIN

Our children must never lose their zeal for building a better world.

MARY MCLEOD BETHUNE

Children are the hands by which we take hold of heaven.

HENRY WARD BEECHER

A TIMELY TIP

Taking care of children is demanding, time-consuming, energy-depleting . . . and profoundly rewarding. Don't ever overlook the rewards.

DEAR MOM,
On the Lines Below, Write Down Your Own Ideas About Children

AND FINALLY . . .

DID YOU KNOW?

In the United States, there are more than 80,000,000 mothers.

CHAPTER 24

DETOURS ON THE JOURNEY

We are pressured in every way but not crushed;
we are perplexed but not in despair.

—

2 CORINTHIANS 4:8 HCSB

When life unfolds according to our wishes, or when we experience unexpected good fortune, we find it easy to praise God's plan. That's when we greet change with open arms. But sometimes the changes that we must endure are painful. When we struggle through the difficult days of life, as we must from time to time, we may ask ourselves, "Why me?" The answer, of course, is that God knows, but He isn't telling . . . yet.

Have you endured a difficult transition that has left your head spinning or your heart broken? If so, you have a clear choice to make: either you can cry and complain, or you can trust God and get busy fixing what's broken. The former is a formula for disaster; the latter is a formula for a well-lived life. So, Mom, with no further delay, let the fretting cease, and let the fixing begin.

MORE GREAT IDEAS ABOUT
ADVERSITY

Faith is a strong power, mastering any difficulty in the strength of the Lord who made heaven and earth.

CORRIE TEN BOOM

If all struggles and sufferings were eliminated, the spirit would no more reach maturity than would the child.

ELISABETH ELLIOT

God will never let you sink under your circumstances. He always provides a safety net and His love always encircles.

BARBARA JOHNSON

Measure the size of the obstacles against the size of God.

BETH MOORE

Even in the winter, even in the midst of the storm, the sun is still there. Somewhere, up above the clouds, it still shines and warms and pulls at the life buried deep inside the brown branches and frozen earth. The sun is there! Spring will come.

GLORIA GAITHER

When faced with adversity the Christian woman comforts herself with the knowledge that all of life's events are in the hands of God.

VONETTE BRIGHT

When problems threaten to engulf us, we must do what believers have always done, turn to the Lord for encouragement and solace. As Psalm 46:1 states, "God is our refuge and strength, an ever-present help in trouble."

SHIRLEY DOBSON

God helps those who help themselves, but there are times when we are quite incapable of helping ourselves. That's when God stoops down and gathers us in His arms like a mother lifts a sick child, and does for us what we cannot do for ourselves.

RUTH BELL GRAHAM

Faith not only can help you through a crisis; it can help you to approach life after the hard times with a whole new perspective. It can help you adopt an outlook of hope and courage through faith-to-face reality.

JOHN MAXWELL

MORE WISDOM FROM GOD'S WORD

I will be with you when you pass through the waters . . . when you walk through the fire . . . the flame will not burn you. For I the Lord your God, the Holy One of Israel, and your Savior.

ISAIAH 43:2-3 HCSB

Consider it a great joy, my brothers, whenever you experience various trials, knowing that the testing of your faith produces endurance. But endurance must do its complete work, so that you may be mature and complete, lacking nothing.

JAMES 1:2-4 HCSB

When you are in distress and all these things have happened to you, you will return to the Lord your God in later days and obey Him. He will not leave you, destroy you, or forget the covenant with your fathers that He swore to them by oath, because the Lord your God is a compassionate God.

DEUTERONOMY 4:30-31 HCSB

But as for you, you meant evil against me; but God meant it for good, in order to bring it about as it is this day, to save many people alive.

GENESIS 50:20 NKJV

HAVE COURAGE

Life can be difficult and discouraging at times. During our darkest moments, we can depend upon our friends and family, and upon God. When we do, we find the courage to face even the darkest days with hopeful hearts and willing hands.

Eleanor Roosevelt advised, "You gain strength, courage, and confidence by every great experience in which you really stop to look fear in the face. You are able to say to yourself, 'I lived through this horror. I can take the next thing that comes along.' You must do the thing you think you cannot do."

So the next time you find your courage tested to the limit, remember that you're probably stronger than you think. And remember—with you, your friends, your family, and your God all working together, you have nothing to fear.

MORE GOOD IDEAS

Jesus Christ can make the weakest man into a divine dreadnought, fearing nothing.

OSWALD CHAMBERS

Fill your mind with thoughts of God rather than thoughts of fear.

NORMAN VINCENT PEALE

When once we are assured that God is good, then there can be nothing left to fear.

HANNAH WHITALL SMITH

A TIMELY TIP

If you're facing big-time adversity, don't hit the panic button and don't keep everything bottled up inside. Instead of going underground, talk things over with your husband, with your friends, with your pastor, and if necessary, with a trained counselor. When it comes to navigating the stormy seas of life, second, third, fourth, or even fifth opinions can sometimes be helpful.

DEAR MOM,
On the Lines Below, Write Down Your Own Ideas About Overcoming Tough Times

_____

_____

_____

_____

_____

_____

_____

_____

_____

_____

_____

_____

_____

_____

_____

_____

_____

_____

_____

_____

_____

And Finally . . .

Did You Know?

According to AT&T, Mother's Day
is the #1 holiday for long-distance phone calls.

CHAPTER 25

THE RIGHT KIND OF EXAMPLE

*You should be an example to the believers in speech,
in conduct, in love, in faith, in purity.*

—

1 TIMOTHY 4:12 HCSB

Our children learn from the lessons we teach and the lives we live, but not necessarily in that order. As mothers, we serve as unforgettable role models for our children and grandchildren. Hopefully, the lives we lead and the choices we make will serve as enduring examples of the spiritual abundance that is available to all who worship God and obey His commandments.

What kind of example are you? Are you the kind of mother whose life serves as a genuine example of patience and righteousness? Are you a woman whose behavior serves as a positive role model for others? Are you the kind of mom whose actions, day in and day out, are based upon kindness, faithfulness, and a sincere love for the Lord? If so, you are not only blessed by God, but you are also a powerful force for good in a world that desperately needs positive influences such as yours.

Corrie ten Boom advised, "Don't worry about what you do not understand. Worry about what you do understand in the Bible but do not live by." And that's sound advice because our families and friends are watching . . . and so, for that matter, is God.

MORE GREAT IDEAS ABOUT EXAMPLE

A true mother is not merely a provider, housekeeper, comforter, or companion. A true mother is primarily and essentially a trainer.

RUTH BELL GRAHAM

Mothers must model the tenderness we need. Our world can't find it anywhere else.

CHARLES SWINDOLL

Living life with a consistent spiritual walk deeply influences those we love most.

VONETTE BRIGHT

Every home is a school. What are you going to teach today?

MARIE T. FREEMAN

Whether we signed up for the responsibility or not, Christian parents give their children impressions of what they can expect from God.

Beth Moore

In serving we uncover the greatest fulfillment within and become a stellar example of a woman who knows and loves Jesus.

Vonette Bright

Each one of us is God's special work of art. Through us, He teaches and inspires, delights and encourages, informs and uplifts all those who view our lives. God, the master artist, is most concerned about expressing Himself—His thoughts and His intentions—through what He paints in our character . . . . [He] wants to paint a beautiful portrait of His Son in and through your life. A painting like no other in all of time.

Joni Eareckson Tada

Let us preach you, Dear Jesus, without preaching, not by words but by our example, by the casting force, the sympathetic influence of what we do, the evident fullness of the love our hearts bear to you. Amen.

Mother Teresa

MORE WISDOM FROM GOD'S WORD

Do everything without grumbling and arguing, so that you may be blameless and pure.

PHILIPPIANS 2:14–15 HCSB

Set an example of good works yourself, with integrity and dignity in your teaching.

TITUS 2:7 HCSB

For the kingdom of God is not in talk but in power.

1 CORINTHIANS 4:20 HCSB

Therefore since we also have such a large cloud of witnesses surrounding us, let us lay aside every weight and the sin that so easily ensnares us, and run with endurance the race that lies before us.

HEBREWS 12:1 HCSB

You are the light of the world. A city situated on a hill cannot be hidden.

MATTHEW 5:14 HCSB

Doing What's Right

Life is a series of choices. Each day, we make countless decisions that can bring us closer to God . . . or not. When we live according to God's commandments, we earn for ourselves the abundance and peace that He intends for our lives. But, when we turn our backs upon God by disobeying Him, we bring needless suffering upon ourselves and our families.

Do you seek God's peace and His blessings? Then obey Him. When you're faced with a difficult choice or a powerful temptation, seek God's counsel and trust the counsel He gives. Invite God into your heart and live according to His commandments. When you do, you will be blessed today and tomorrow and forever.

MORE GOOD IDEAS

Every day, I find countless opportunities to decide whether I will obey God and demonstrate my love for Him or try to please myself or the world system. God is waiting for my choices.

BILL BRIGHT

Every time you make a choice, you are turning the central part of you, the part that chooses, into something a little different from what it was before.

C. S. LEWIS

God always gives His best to those who leave the choice with Him.

JIM ELLIOT

A TIMELY TIP

Your children will learn about life from many sources; the most important source should be you. But remember that the lectures you give are never as important as the ones you live.

DEAR MOM,
On the Lines Below, Write Down Your Own Ideas About
The Rewards of Doing the Right Thing

And Finally . . .

Parents can tell but never teach,
until they practice what they preach.

CHAPTER 26

THE POWER OF ENCOURAGEMENT

I want their hearts to be encouraged and joined together in love,
so that they may have all the riches of assured understanding,
and have the knowledge of God's mystery—Christ.

—

COLOSSIANS 2:2 HCSB

Life is a team sport, and all of us need occasional pats on the back from our teammates. Whether you realize it or not, many of the people you encounter each day are in desperate need of a smile or an encouraging word. The world can be a difficult place, and countless friends and family members may be troubled by the challenges of everyday life.

Since you don't always know who needs our help, the best strategy is to try to encourage all the people who cross your path. So here's something you can do, Mom: Today, make this promise to yourself and keep it: vow to be a world-class source of encouragement to everyone you meet. Share your optimism with family members, friends, coworkers, and even with strangers. Never has the need been greater.

MORE GREAT IDEAS ABOUT
ENCOURAGEMENT

Always stay connected to people and seek out things that bring you joy. Dream with abandon. Pray confidently.

BARBARA JOHNSON

The glory of friendship is not the outstretched hand or the kindly smile or the joy of companionship. It is the spiritual inspiration that comes to one when he discovers that someone else believes in him and is willing to trust him with his friendship.

CORRIE TEN BOOM

Encouragement starts at home, but it should never end there.

MARIE T. FREEMAN

If I am asked how we are to get rid of discouragements, I can only say, as I have had to say of so many other wrong spiritual habits, we must give them up. It is never worthwhile to argue against discouragement. There is only one argument that can meet it, and that is the argument of God.

HANNAH WHITALL SMITH

A single word, if spoken in a friendly spirit, may be sufficient to turn one from dangerous error.

FANNY CROSBY

Don't forget that a single sentence, spoken at the right moment, can change somebody's whole perspective on life. A little encouragement can go a long, long way.

MARIE T. FREEMAN

Words. Do you fully understand their power? Can any of us really grasp the mighty force behind the things we say? Do we stop and think before we speak, considering the potency of the words we utter?

JONI EARECKSON TADA

One of the ways God refills us after failure is through the blessing of Christian fellowship. Just experiencing the joy of simple activities shared with other children of God can have a healing effect on us.

ANNE GRAHAM LOTZ

How many people stop because so few say, "Go!"

CHARLES SWINDOLL

MORE WISDOM FROM GOD'S WORD

Carry one another's burdens; in this way you will fulfill the law of Christ.

GALATIANS 6:2 HCSB

But encourage each other daily, while it is still called today, so that none of you is hardened by sin's deception.

HEBREWS 3:13 HCSB

And let us be concerned about one another in order to promote love and good works.

HEBREWS 10:24 HCSB

Anxiety in a man's heart weighs it down, but a good word cheers it up.

PROVERBS 12:25 HCSB

So then, we must pursue what promotes peace and what builds up one another.

ROMANS 14:19 HCSB

THE POWER OF GENUINE FRIENDSHIP

What is a friend? The dictionary defines the word "friend" as "a person who is attached to another by feelings of affection or personal regard." This definition is accurate, as far as it goes, but when we examine the deeper meaning of friendship, so many more descriptors come to mind: trustworthiness, loyalty, helpfulness, kindness, understanding, forgiveness, encouragement, humor, and cheerfulness, to mention but a few.

Genuine friendship should be treasured and nourished. As Christians, we are governed by the Golden Rule: we are commanded to treat others as we wish to be treated. When we treat others with kindness, courtesy, and respect, we build friendships that can last a lifetime. And God smiles.

MORE GOOD IDEAS

Friendships are living organisms at work. They continue to unfold, change, and emerge.

BARBARA JOHNSON

Friendship is something that raised us almost above humanity. This love, free from instinct, free from all duties but those which love has freely assumed, almost wholly free from jealousy, and free without qualification from the need to be needed, is eminently spiritual. It is the sort of love one can imagine between angels.

C. S. LEWIS

My special friends, who know me so well and love me anyway, give me daily encouragement to keep on.

EMILIE BARNES

A TIMELY TIP

Encouragement is contagious. You can't lift other people up without lifting yourself up, too.

DEAR MOM,
On the Lines Below, Write Down Your Own Ideas About The Importance of Encouragement

AND FINALLY . . .

THE BEST WAY TO KNOCK THE CHIP
OFF YOUR NEIGHBOR'S SHOULDER
IS TO PAT HIM ON THE BACK.

THE POWER
OF ENTHUSIASM

Whatever you do, do it enthusiastically,
as something done for the Lord and not for men.

—

COLOSSIANS 3:23 HCSB

Enthusiasm, like other human emotions, is contagious. If you associate with hope-filled, enthusiastic people, their enthusiasm will have a tendency to lift your spirits. But if you find yourself spending too much time in the company of naysayers, pessimists, or cynics, your thoughts, like theirs, will tend to be negative.

So, Mom, as you consider ways to improve your spiritual and emotional health, ask yourself if you're associating with positive people. If so, then you can rest assured you're availing yourself of a priceless gift: encouragement.

Today, look for reasons to celebrate God's countless blessings. And while you're at it, look for upbeat friends who will join with you in the celebration. You'll be better for their company, and they'll be better for yours.

MORE GREAT IDEAS ABOUT ENTHUSIASM

God is the giver, and we are the receivers. And His richest gifts are bestowed not upon those who do the greatest things, but upon those who accept His abundance and His grace.

HANNAH WHITALL SMITH

Living life with a consistent spiritual walk deeply influences those we love most.

VONETTE BRIGHT

Your light is the truth of the Gospel message itself as well as your witness as to who Jesus is and what He has done for you. Don't hide it.

ANNE GRAHAM LOTZ

Making up a string of excuses is usually harder than doing the work.

MARIE T. FREEMAN

We urgently need people who encourage and inspire us to move toward God and away from the world's enticing pleasures.

JIM CYMBALA

Enthusiasm, like the flu, is contagious—we get it from one another.

Barbara Johnson

Wouldn't it make astounding difference, not only in the quality of the work we do, but also in the satisfaction, even our joy, if we recognized God's gracious gift in every single task?

Elisabeth Elliot

I don't know about you, but I want to do more than survive life—I want to mount up like the eagle and glide over rocky crags, nest in the tallest of trees, dive for nourishment in the deepest of mountain lakes, and soar on the wings of the wind.

Barbara Johnson

Prayer must be aflame. Prayer without fervor is as a sun without light or heat, or as a flower without beauty or fragrance. A soul devoted to God is a fervent soul, and prayer is the creature of that flame. He only can truly pray who is all aglow for holiness, for God, and for heaven.

E. M. Bounds

MORE WISDOM FROM GOD'S WORD

I have seen that there is nothing better than for a person to enjoy his activities, because that is his reward. For who can enable him to see what will happen after he dies?

ECCLESIASTES 3:22 HCSB

Do not lack diligence; be fervent in spirit; serve the Lord.

ROMANS 12:11 HCSB

He did it with all his heart. So he prospered.

2 CHRONICLES 31:21 NKJV

This is the day the Lord has made; let us rejoice and be glad in it.

PSALM 118:24 HCSB

Render service with a good attitude, as to the Lord and not to men.

EPHESIANS 6:7 HCSB

MORE GOOD IDEAS

Get absolutely enthralled with something. Throw yourself into it with abandon. Get out of yourself. Be somebody. Do something.

NORMAN VINCENT PEALE

It is a remarkable thing that some of the most optimistic and enthusiastic people you will meet are those who have been through intense suffering.

WARREN WIERSBE

We act as though comfort and luxury were the chief requirements of life, when all we need to make us really happy is something to be enthusiastic about.

CHARLES KINGSLEY

A TIMELY TIP

Don't wait for enthusiasm to find you . . . go looking for it. Look at your life and your relationships as exciting adventures. Don't wait for life to spice itself; spice things up yourself.

DEAR MOM,
On the Lines Below, Write Down Your Own Ideas About Enthusiasm

CHAPTER 28

YOUR SHEPHERD

The Lord is my shepherd; I shall not want.

—

PSALM 23:1 KJV

In the 23rd Psalm, David teaches us that God is like a watchful shepherd caring for His flock, a flock which includes you. You are precious in the eyes of God—you are His priceless creation, made in His image, and protected by Him. God watches over you, and you need never be afraid. But sometimes, fear has a way of slipping into the minds and hearts of even the most devout women—and you are no exception.

As a busy mother, you know from firsthand experience that life is not always easy. But as a recipient of God's grace, you also know that you are protected by a loving Heavenly Father.

Today, be still and listen for the quiet assurance of God's promises. And then, place your life in His hands. He is your shepherd today and throughout eternity. Trust the Shepherd.

MORE GREAT IDEAS ABOUT
GOD'S PROTECTION

God will never let you sink under your circumstances. He always provides a safety net and His love always encircles.

BARBARA JOHNSON

Only believe, don't fear. Our Master, Jesus, always watches over us, and no matter what the persecution, Jesus will surely overcome it.

LOTTIE MOON

Our future may look fearfully intimidating, yet we can look up to the Engineer of the Universe, confident that nothing escapes His attention or slips out of the control of those strong hands.

ELISABETH ELLIOT

Worries carry responsibilities that belong to God, not to you. Worry does not enable us to escape evil; it makes us unfit to cope with it when it comes.

CORRIE TEN BOOM

The Rock of Ages is the great sheltering encirclement.

OSWALD CHAMBERS

We are never out of reach of Satan's devices, so we must never be without the whole armor of God.

WARREN WIERSBE

As sure as God puts his children in the furnace, he will be in the furnace with them.

C. H. SPURGEON

God's promises are medicine for the broken heart. Let Him comfort you. And, after He has comforted you, try to share that comfort with somebody else. It will do both of you good.

WARREN WIERSBE

When we meditate on God and remember the promises He has given us in His Word, our faith grows, and our fears dissolve.

CHARLES STANLEY

A God wise enough to create me and the world I live in is wise enough to watch out for me.

PHILIP YANCEY

MORE WISDOM FROM GOD'S WORD

The LORD is my shepherd; I shall not want. He maketh me to lie down in green pastures: he leadeth me beside the still waters. He restoreth my soul: he leadeth me in the paths of righteousness for his name's sake. Yea, though I walk through the valley of the shadow of death, I will fear no evil: for thou art with me; thy rod and thy staff they comfort me. Thou preparest a table before me in the presence of mine enemies: thou anointest my head with oil; my cup runneth over. Surely goodness and mercy shall follow me all the days of my life: and I will dwell in the house of the LORD for ever.

PSALM 23 KJV

Finally, my brethren, be strong in the Lord and in the power of His might. Put on the whole armor of God, that you may be able to stand against the wiles of the devil.

EPHESIANS 6:10-11 NKJV

The Lord your God in your midst, The Mighty One, will save; He will rejoice over you with gladness, He will quiet you with His love, He will rejoice over you with singing.

ZEPHANIAH 3:17 NKJV

I know whom I have believed and am persuaded that He is able to guard what has been entrusted to me until that day.

2 TIMOTHY 1:12 HCSB

TRUST GOD

Sometimes the future seems bright, and sometimes it does not. Yet even when we cannot see the possibilities of tomorrow, God can. As believers, our challenge is to trust an uncertain future to an all-powerful God.

When we trust God, we should trust Him without reservation. We should steel ourselves against the inevitable disappointments of the day, secure in the knowledge that our Heavenly Father has a plan for the future that only He can see.

Can you place your future into the hands of a loving and all-knowing God? Can you live amid the uncertainties of today, knowing that God has dominion over all your tomorrows? If you can, you are wise and you are blessed. When you trust God with everything you are and everything you have, He will bless you now and forever.

MORE GOOD IDEAS

Trusting in my own mental understanding becomes a hindrance to complete trust in God.

OSWALD CHAMBERS

God has proven himself as a faithful father. Now it falls to us to be trusting children.

MAX LUCADO

Never be afraid to trust an unknown future to a known God.

CORRIE TEN BOOM

A TIMELY TIP

You are protected by God . . . now and always. The only security that lasts is the security that flows from the loving heart of God.

DEAR MOM,
On the Lines Below, Write Down Your Own Ideas About God's Protection

And Finally . . .

Never be afraid to hope—
or to ask God—
for a miracle.

CHAPTER 29

BELIEVE IN YOURSELF!

*For You have made him a little lower than the angels,
And You have crowned him with glory and honor.*

—

PSALM 8:5 NKJV

Mom, do you place a high value on your talents, your time, your capabilities, and your opportunities? If so, congratulations. But if you've acquired the insidious habit of devaluing your time, your work, or yourself, it's now time for a change. So if you've unintentionally been squandering opportunities or somehow selling yourself short, please do your yourself and your loved ones a favor by rethinking the way that you think about yourself (got that?).

No one can seize opportunities for you, and no one can build up your self-confidence if you're unwilling to believe in yourself. So if you've been talking disrespectfully to yourself, stop; if you've been underestimating your talents, cease. You deserve better treatment from yourself . . . far better. And if you don't give yourself healthy respect, who will?

MORE GREAT IDEAS ABOUT
SELF-ESTEEM

Being loved by Him whose opinion matters most gives us the security to risk loving, too—even loving ourselves.

GLORIA GAITHER

Give yourself a gift today: be present with yourself. God is. Enjoy your own personality. God does.

BARBARA JOHNSON

The Creator has made us each one of a kind. There is nobody else exactly like us, and there never will be. Each of us is his special creation and is alive for a distinctive purpose.

LUCI SWINDOLL

Comparison is the root of all feelings of inferiority.

JAMES DOBSON

When it comes to our position before God, we're perfect. When he sees each of us, he sees one who has been made perfect through the One who is perfect—Jesus Christ.

MAX LUCADO

I was learning something important: we are most vulnerable to the piercing winds of doubt when we distance ourselves from the mission and fellowship to which Christ has called us. Our night of discouragement will seem endless and our task impossible, unless we recognize that He stands in our midst.

JONI EARECKSON TADA

It is not enough to love ourselves; we must also like ourselves.

JOYCE MEYER

Your core identity—and particularly your perception of it—plays a vital role in determining how you carry yourself in daily life, how much joy you experience, how you treat other people, and how you respond to God.

JOSH MCDOWELL

Your self worth is more important than your net worth.

ANONYMOUS

MORE WISDOM FROM GOD'S WORD

You're blessed when you're content with just who you are—no more, no less. That's the moment you find yourselves proud owners of everything that can't be bought.

MATTHEW 5:5 MSG

A devout life does bring wealth, but it's the rich simplicity of being yourself before God.

1 TIMOTHY 6:6 MSG

You made all the delicate, inner parts of my body and knit me together in my mother's womb. Thank you for making me so wonderfully complex! Your workmanship is marvelous—and how well I know it.

PSALM 139:13-14 NLT

My dear children, let's not just talk about love; let's practice real love. This is the only way we'll know we're living truly, living in God's reality. It's also the way to shut down debilitating self-criticism, even when there is something to it. For God is greater than our worried hearts and knows more about us than we do ourselves. And friends, once that's taken care of and we're no longer accusing or condemning ourselves, we're bold and free before God!

1 JOHN 3:18-21 MSG

MORE GOOD IDEAS

Attitude is the mind's paintbrush; it can color any situation.

BARBARA JOHNSON

God knows all that is true about us and is a friend to the face we show and the face we hide. He does not love us less for our human weaknesses.

SHEILA WALSH

I think that if God forgives us we might forgive ourselves. Otherwise it is almost like setting up ourselves as a higher tribunal than Him.

C. S. LEWIS

A TIMELY TIP

Your family's collective self-esteem starts at the head of the household and works its way down from there. It's not enough to concern yourself with your child's self-image; you should also strive to become comfortable with your own self-image, too.

DEAR MOM,
On the Lines Below, Write Down Your Own Ideas About Self-Esteem

ABOVE AND BEYOND WORRY

Don't worry about your life, what you will eat
or what you will drink; or about your body, what you will wear.
Isn't life more than food and the body more than clothing?

—

MATTHEW 6:25 HCSB

If you are like most mothers, it is simply a fact of life: from time to time, you worry. You worry about children, about health, about finances, about safety, and about countless other challenges of life, some great and some small. Where is the best place to take your worries? Take them to God. Take your troubles to Him and your fears and your sorrows.

Barbara Johnson correctly observed, "Worry is the senseless process of cluttering up tomorrow's opportunities with leftover problems from today." So if you'd like to make the most out of this day (and every one hereafter), turn your worries over to a Power greater than yourself . . . and spend your valuable time and energy solving the problems you can fix . . . while trusting God to do the rest.

MORE GREAT IDEAS ABOUT WORRY

We are not called to be burden-bearers, but cross-bearers and light-bearers. We must cast our burdens on the Lord.

CORRIE TEN BOOM

This life of faith, then, consists in just this—being a child in the Father's house. Let the ways of childish confidence and freedom from care, which so please you and win your heart when you observe your own little ones, teach you what you should be in your attitude toward God.

HANNAH WHITALL SMITH

Never yield to gloomy anticipation. Place your hope and confidence in God. He has no record of failure.

MRS. CHARLES E. COWMAN

It is not work that's kills, but worry. And, it is amazing how much wear and tear the human mind and spirit can stand if it is free from friction and well-oiled by the Spirit.

VANCE HAVNER

Worry makes you forget who's in charge.

MAX LUCADO

Worry is a cycle of inefficient thoughts whirling around a center of fear.

CORRIE TEN BOOM

When there is perplexity there is always guidance—not always at the moment we ask, but in good time, which is God's time. There is no need to fret and stew.

ELISABETH ELLIOT

Anxiety may be natural and normal for the world, but it is not to be part of a believer's lifestyle.

KAY ARTHUR

Today is mine. Tomorrow is none of my business. If I peer anxiously into the fog of the future, I will strain my spiritual eyes so that I will not see clearly what is required of me now.

ELISABETH ELLIOTT

When God is at the center of your life, you worship. When he's not, you worry.

RICK WARREN

MORE WISDOM FROM GOD'S WORD

Don't worry about anything, but in everything, through prayer and petition with thanksgiving, let your requests be made known to God.

PHILIPPIANS 4:6 HCSB

Therefore don't worry about tomorrow, because tomorrow will worry about itself. Each day has enough trouble of its own.

MATTHEW 6:34 HCSB

Yea, though I walk through the valley of the shadow of death, I will fear no evil: for thou art with me; thy rod and thy staff they comfort me.

PSALM 23:4 KJV

I will be with you when you pass through the waters . . . when you walk through the fire . . . the flame will not burn you. For I the Lord your God, the Holy One of Israel, and your Savior.

ISAIAH 43:2-3 HCSB

Those who trust in the Lord are like Mount Zion. It cannot be shaken; it remains forever.

PSALM 125:1 HCSB

NOBODY'S PERFECT

We are imperfect people living in an imperfect world; mistakes are simply part of the price we pay for being here. But, even though mistakes are an inevitable part of life's journey, repeated mistakes should not be. When we commit the inevitable blunders of life, we must correct them, learn from them, and pray to God for the wisdom not to repeat them. And then, if we are successful, our mistakes become lessons, and our lives become adventures in growth, not stagnation.

So Mom, the next time you experience one of life's inevitable setbacks, it's time to start looking for the lesson that God is trying to teach you. It's time to learn what needs to be learned, change what needs to be changed, and move on.

MORE GOOD IDEAS

Mistakes offer the possibility for redemption and a new start in God's kingdom. No matter what you're guilty of, God can restore your innocence.

BARBARA JOHNSON

God is able to take mistakes, when they are committed to Him, and make of them something for our good and for His glory.

RUTH BELL GRAHAM

No matter how badly we have failed, we can always get up and begin again. Our God is the God of new beginnings.

WARREN WIERSBE

A TIMELY TIP

No parent is perfect, not even you. So when you make mistakes, as you most certainly will from time to time, ask for forgiveness, especially if you're seeking it from your kids. Your behavior will serve as a priceless example to your children.

DEAR MOM,
On the Lines Below, Write Down Your Own Ideas About Learning from Mistakes

AND FINALLY . . .

Mother's Day is now celebrated in many countries around the world. Australia, Mexico, Denmark, Finland, Italy, Turkey, Belgium, Russia, China, Thailand, all have special celebrations that honor moms.

CHAPTER 31

QUIET TIME WITH GOD

Be still, and know that I am God . . . .

—

PSALM 46:10 KJV

We live in a noisy world, a world filled with distractions, frustrations, obligations, and complications. But we must not allow our clamorous world to separate us from God's peace. Instead, we must "be still" so that we might sense the presence of God.

If we are to maintain righteous minds and compassionate hearts, we must take time each day for prayer and for meditation. We must make ourselves still in the presence of our Creator. We must quiet our minds and our hearts so that we might sense God's love, God's will, and God's Son.

Has the busy pace of life robbed you of the peace that might otherwise be yours through Jesus Christ? If so, it's time to reorder your priorities. Nothing is more important than the time you spend with your Savior. So be still and claim the inner peace that is your spiritual birthright: the peace of Jesus Christ. It is offered freely; it has been paid for in full; it is yours for the asking. So ask. And then share.

MORE GREAT IDEAS ABOUT
STILLNESS

Let your loneliness be transformed into a holy aloneness. Sit still before the Lord. Remember Naomi's word to Ruth: "Sit still, my daughter, until you see how the matter will fall."

ELISABETH ELLIOT

Because Jesus Christ is our Great High Priest, not only can we approach God without a human "go-between," we can also hear and learn from God in some sacred moments without one.

BETH MOORE

When we are in the presence of God, removed from distractions, we are able to hear him more clearly, and a secure environment has been established for the young and broken places in our hearts to surface.

JOHN ELDREDGE

Instead of waiting for the feeling, wait upon God. You can do this by growing still and quiet, then expressing in prayer what your mind knows is true about Him, even if your heart doesn't feel it at this moment.

SHIRLEY DOBSON

It is in that stillness that the Voice will be heard, the only voice in all the universe that speaks peace to the deepest part of us.

ELISABETH ELLIOT

Be quiet enough to hear God's whisper.

ANONYMOUS

I need the spiritual revival that comes from spending quiet time alone with Jesus in prayer and in thoughtful meditation on His Word.

ANNE GRAHAM LOTZ

The moment you wake up each morning, all your wishes and hopes for the day rush at you like wild animals. And the first job each morning consists in shoving it all back; in listening to that other voice, taking that other point of view, letting that other, larger, stronger, quieter life coming flowing in.

C. S. LEWIS

What digestion is to the body, meditation is to the soul.

WARREN WIERSBE

MORE WISDOM FROM GOD'S WORD

In quietness and trust is your strength.

ISAIAH 30:15 NASB

What's this? Fools out shopping for wisdom! They wouldn't recognize it if they saw it!

PROVERBS 17:16 MSG

I wait quietly before God, for my hope is in him.

PSALM 62:5 NLT

Morning by morning he wakens me and opens my understanding to his will. The Sovereign Lord has spoken to me, and I have listened.

ISAIAH 50:4-5 NLT

Be silent before Me.

ISAIAH 41:1 HCSB

FINDING PEACE IN THE STORM

A frightening storm rose quickly on the Sea of Galilee, and the disciples were afraid. Because of their limited faith, they feared for their lives. When they turned to Jesus, He calmed the waters and He rebuked His disciples for their lack of faith in Him.

On occasion, we, like the disciples, are frightened by the inevitable storms of life. Why are we afraid? Because we, like the disciples, possess imperfect faith.

When we genuinely accept God's promises as absolute truth, when we trust Him with life here on earth and life eternal, we have little to fear. Faith in God is the antidote to worry. Faith in God is the foundation of courage and the source of power. Today, let us trust God more completely and, by doing so, move beyond our fears to a place of abundance, assurance, and peace.

MORE GOOD IDEAS

In the center of a hurricane there is absolute quiet and peace. There is no safer place than in the center of the will of God.

CORRIE TEN BOOM

For Jesus peace seems to have meant not the absence of struggle but the presence of love.

FREDERICK BUECHNER

The fruit of our placing all things in God's hands is the presence of His abiding peace in our hearts.

HANNAH WHITALL SMITH

A TIMELY TIP

Do you want to discover God's peace? Then do your best to live in the center of God's will.

DEAR MOM,
On the Lines Below, Write Down Your Own Ideas About Ways to Live a More Peaceful Life

And Finally . . .

No Jesus, no peace;
Know Jesus, know peace!

CHAPTER 32

EMBRACED BY GOD

For God so loved the world, that he gave his only begotten Son,
that whosoever believeth in him should not perish,
but have everlasting life.

—

JOHN 3:16 KJV

As a mother, you know the profound love that you hold in your heart for your own children. As a child of God, you can only imagine the infinite love that your Heavenly Father holds for you.

God made you in His own image and gave you salvation through the person of His Son Jesus Christ. And now, precisely because you are a wondrous creation treasured by God, a question presents itself: What will you do in response to the Creator's love? Will you ignore it or embrace it? Will you return it or neglect it? That decision, of course, is yours and yours alone.

When you embrace God's love, you are forever changed. When you embrace God's love, you feel differently about yourself, your neighbors, your family, and your world. More importantly, you share God's message—and His love—with others.

Your Heavenly Father—a God of infinite love and mercy—is waiting to embrace you with open arms.

MORE GREAT IDEAS ABOUT GOD'S LOVE

God wants to reveal Himself as your heavenly Father. When you are hurting, you can run to Him and crawl up into His lap. When you wonder which way to turn, you can grasp His strong hand, and He'll guide you along life's path. When everything around you is falling apart, you'll feel your Father's arm around your shoulder to hold you together.

LISA WHELCHEL

Snuggle in God's arms. When you are hurting, when you feel lonely or left out, let Him cradle you, comfort you, reassure you of His all-sufficient power and love.

KAY ARTHUR

The fact is, God no longer deals with us in judgment but in mercy. If people got what they deserved, this old planet would have ripped apart at the seams centuries ago. Praise God that because of His great love "we are not consumed, for his compassions never fail" (Lam. 3:22).

JONI EARECKSON TADA

Being loved by Him whose opinion matters most gives us the security to risk loving, too—even loving ourselves.

GLORIA GAITHER

There is no pit so deep that God's love is not deeper still.

CORRIE TEN BOOM

Jesus loves us with fidelity, purity, constancy, and passion, no matter how imperfect we are.

STORMIE OMARTIAN

Accepting God's love as a gift instead of trying to earn it had somehow seemed presumptuous and arrogant to me, when, in fact, my pride was tricking me into thinking that I could merit His love and forgiveness with my own strength.

LISA WHELCHEL

God is a God of unconditional, unremitting love, a love that corrects and chastens but never ceases.

KAY ARTHUR

Even when we cannot see the why and wherefore of God's dealings, we know that there is love in and behind them, so we can rejoice always.

J. I. PACKER

MORE WISDOM FROM GOD'S WORD

For the Lord is good, and His love is eternal; His faithfulness endures through all generations.

PSALM 100:5 HCSB

[Because of] the Lord's faithful love we do not perish, for His mercies never end. They are new every morning; great is Your faithfulness!

LAMENTATIONS 3:22-23 HCSB

Help me, Lord my God; save me according to Your faithful love.

PSALM 109:26 HCSB

Whoever is wise will observe these things, and they will understand the lovingkindness of the Lord.

PSALM 107:43 NKJV

A person's insight gives him patience, and his virtue is to overlook an offense.

PROVERBS 19:11 HCSB

FOR GOD SO LOVED THE WORLD

How much does God love you? To answer that question, you need only to look at the cross. God's love for you is so great that He sent His only Son to this earth to die for your sins and to offer you the priceless gift of eternal life.

You must decide whether or not to accept God's gift. Will you ignore it or embrace it? Will you return it or neglect it? Will you invite Christ to dwell in the center of your heart, or will you relegate Him to a position of lesser importance? The decision is yours, and so are the consequences. So choose wisely . . . and choose today.

More Good Ideas

Teach us to set our hopes on heaven, to hold firmly to the promise of eternal life, so that we can withstand the struggles and storms of this world.

Max Lucado

And because we know Christ is alive, we have hope for the present and hope for life beyond the grave.

Billy Graham

Once a man is united to God, how could he not live forever? Once a man is separated from God, what can he do but wither and die?

C. S. Lewis

A Timely Tip

God offers you a priceless gift: the gift of eternal life. If you have not already done so, accept God's gift today—tomorrow may be too late.

DEAR MOM,
On the Lines Below, Write Down Your Own Ideas About God's Eternal Gifts

And Finally . . .

BIBLE:

Basic
Instructions
Before
Leaving
Earth